the CDA *Prep Guide*

the CDA *Prep* Guide

The Complete Review Manual
for the Child Development
Associate Credential

SECOND EDITION

DEBRA PIERCE

Redleaf Press®
www.redleafpress.org
800-423-8309

Published by Redleaf Press
10 Yorkton Court
St. Paul, MN 55117
www.redleafpress.org

First edition published 2008. Second edition 2011.
Cover design by Jim Handrigan
Interior design by David Farr and typeset in SabonNext
Printed in the United States of America
18 17 16 15 14 13 12 11   1 2 3 4 5 6 7 8

The CDA Competency Goal Statements and Functional Areas referenced throughout the book, the CDA Subject Areas chart on page 179, and the glossary on pages 188–192 were reproduced from *The Child Development Associate Assessment System and Competency Standards* books with permission from the Council for Professional Recognition (www.cdacouncil.org).

Library of Congress Cataloging-in-Publication Data
Pierce, Debra, 1949-
   The CDA prep guide : the complete review manual for the child development
associate credential / Debra Pierce. — 2nd ed.
      p. cm.
   Includes bibliographical references and index.
    ISBN 978-1-60554-105-1 (alk. paper)
    1. Child care workers—Certification—United States. 2. Child care
workers—Training of—United States. 3. Child care workers—Employment—
United States. 4. Early childhood education—United States.   I. Title.
HQ778.63.P54 2008
362.71'2076—dc23
                                                                    2011027817

Contents

Introduction

IF YOU ARE CONSIDERING OR WORKING TOWARD your Child Development Associate (CDA) Credential, you are to be commended! The early care and education of young children is a profession, and becoming a professional takes commitment and a desire to do your best to meet the quality standards that define membership in a particular profession.

About the Second Edition

In the interest of providing CDA candidates with the most up-to-date help and information possible, this second edition of *The CDA Prep Guide* reflects recent major updates to *The Child Development Associate Assessment System and Competency Standards* books, two of which are now in their third editions. The Council for Professional Recognition updated these books to reflect a recent review of the national standards on which the CDA assessment is based. Most notably, the Functional Areas within the Competency Goals have been updated to reflect the most current research about best practices and child development. The basic Competency Goals themselves, however, have not changed. The revised Competency Standards books also contain a new section on dual-language learners that includes research-based Developmental Contexts and examples of strategies that caregivers can use in their programs.

In addition to the changes to the Competency Standards books, this second edition of *The CDA Prep Guide* includes information about recent changes to the Council's application procedures and other tips to help make understanding of the CDA process even easier.

Pursuing a CDA Credential

CDA candidates have varying amounts of child care training through college classes, in-service training, or attendance at a variety of workshops. Many of you are working on a degree or have already earned a degree in a related area of study. If you are new to the field, you may be just beginning to learn about child development and educating young children through your CDA training hours.

The reasons early child care and education providers are interested in pursuing a CDA Credential are as varied as the backgrounds they bring to their work. Some providers already working in the field may need to earn a CDA Credential to retain a position, to advance to lead teaching positions, or to become directors. Others just entering the field may need a CDA Credential to be considered for a position.

New research continues to show the importance of the early years in terms of children's development and offers strong motivation to provide quality care and education in early childhood programs. The only way to accomplish this is to ensure that care providers meet nationally recognized standards.

The CDA program provides the means to assess and credential child care providers on the basis of their work with young children, in their particular workplace setting, with the age group of children they teach. The CDA program is administered by the Council for Professional Recognition headquartered in Washington, DC, which is the organization that awards the CDA Credential.

Aside from meeting mandates or enhancing personal marketability, going through the CDA process will reward you with confidence and new insight into working with young children. This process will also provide a sense of personal satisfaction in knowing you have the knowledge and tools to do your professional best in your career.

This book simplifies the required tasks of CDA documentation and assessment into a step-by-step process. Whether you are a center-based caregiver, family child care provider, center director, or potential early childhood professional, this book will help you understand and complete the CDA process. You may be in a formal CDA preparatory program or you may be working on your own. Whichever the case, I hope you'll find the easy-to-understand answers, suggestions, and support helpful in your pursuit of the CDA Credential.

As you begin to take the steps required to earn your CDA Credential, you will need to complete 120 clock hours of training, gather documentation, submit the application, and participate in the verification visit with the Council representative. When you've successfully completed these steps, your abilities as a primary care and education provider for young children will be substantiated by this professional, nationally recognized credential, which is suitable to frame and display. Be prepared to work hard, learn much, and be extremely proud of your accomplishment.

How to Use This Guide

The information in this book is intended to supplement the materials in the application packet you received from the Council for Professional Recognition. It is not intended as a substitute for, nor is it simply another version of, the application materials. If you have not ordered these materials, you will want to do so before beginning to use this book. The materials you receive in the application packet will include two copies of *The Child Development Associate Assessment System and Competency Standards* book, which will vary slightly depending on your particular setting and age-level endorsement. The book has a yellow cover for center-based infant/toddler care, a green cover for center-based preschool care, or a blue cover for family child care. Also in the application packet are the application form, Parent Opinion Questionnaires, the Assessment Observation Instrument, and a copy of the Code of Ethical Conduct from the National Association for the Education of Young Children (NAEYC), all of which will be discussed in detail in this book.

You should be near the end of the required 120 clock hours of formal child care training before you start on the next stages of the CDA assessment.

Not every CDA candidate is working in the same setting or with the same ages of children. For this reason, you do not need to use every section of this book, but only the sections that pertain to your particular situation. Most of the information is of a general nature and is important for all CDA candidates to understand; however, chapter 3 is specific to center-based preschool providers, chapter 4 is specific to center-based infant/toddler providers, and chapter 5 is specific to family child care providers.

When referring to specific text in the CDA books, page numbers are sometimes given to help you find the text. Although unlikely, it is possible that these numbers may change.

Easy-to-understand assistance is provided as you take these steps toward earning your CDA Credential:

- Write your autobiography

- Assemble the Professional Resource Collection for the Professional Resource File

- Compose the six Competency Goal Statements

- Distribute and collect the Parent Opinion Questionnaires

- Select an advisor

- Prepare yourself and your setting for the formal observation by the advisor

- Fill out the Direct Assessment Application form

- Prepare for the verification visit, including practice for the Early Childhood Studies Review exam and the oral interview

After earning your CDA Credential, you can continue to use this book to renew your CDA Credential, get a Second Setting CDA Credential, and decide how to continue your professional development.

Facts about the Child Development Associate (CDA) Credential and Process

What Is a CDA?

CDA stands for Child Development Associate. This is a person who has successfully completed the CDA assessment process and has been awarded the CDA Credential. A person with a CDA Credential has demonstrated the ability to meet the specific needs of children, work with parents and other adults, and promote and nurture children's social, emotional, physical, and intellectual growth in a child development program. The CDA has shown competence in the ability to meet the CDA Competency Goals through work in a center-based, home visitor, family child care, bilingual, or special education setting.

When and how did it all begin?

The Child Development Associate (CDA) National Credentialing Program began in 1971 through the cooperative efforts of the federal government and the early childhood care and education profession in response to concern about the quality of child care in this country. Throughout the 1960s, the number of children in care programs increased dramatically as many mothers entered the workforce, but there was no deliberate and organized effort to keep track of the quality of care that these children were receiving. The quality of care became increasingly important as major research studies at the time indicated how critical the care children receive in the early years is to their subsequent development. The purpose of the program was to assess and credential early childhood care and education professionals on the basis of performance. The program was funded by the U.S. Department of Health and Human Services Administration on Children and Families.

For the first ten years, the CDA program was directed by a coalition of early childhood professional associations, including Bank Street College of Education in New York City. In 1979, the program added Competency Standards and assessment requirements to the system so that candidates in bilingual programs could also be assessed.

At first, the program assessed only workers in center-based preschool programs that served preschool children ages three through five. Between 1985 and 1989, the CDA assessment system was expanded to include caregivers in home visitor and family child care programs and infant/toddler center-based programs.

In the spring of 1985, the National Association for the Education of Young Children (NAEYC) began managing the CDA program. NAEYC set up a separate entity within its organization, called the Council for Professional Recognition, to administer the program nationally. The Council took on complete responsibility for the program beginning in the fall of 1985. As the result of three years of study and review, the Council developed the procedures for assessment and national standards for the delivery of CDA training as we know them today. The Council continues to conduct research on the effectiveness, relevance, and affordability of the credentialing program, periodically making revisions, most recently in 2011.

How many people have the CDA Credential?

Since 1975, the total number of caregivers who have achieved the CDA Credential is over 260,000. As a result of an increased demand for trained and qualified staff by employers in both the public and private sector, well over 18,000 child care providers apply for the CDA Credential each year. In addition, forty-nine states plus the District of Columbia include the CDA Credential as part of their child care licensing regulations.

Who earns a CDA?

More than half of CDAs are between the ages of twenty-six and forty, with an increasing number of CDAs over the age of forty. The majority of people who have earned a CDA are female (Bailey 2004).

Why Is Getting a CDA Important?

Working through the CDA process can be worthwhile and rewarding. In so doing, you can accomplish these goals:

- Earn a nationally recognized credential
- Evaluate your own work as it compares with national standards, and improve on your skills
- Receive one-on-one advice, support, and feedback from early childhood professionals who have knowledge of child development and experience working with young children
- Improve upon your existing skills to the benefit of yourself and the young children in your care

Who Can Apply for a CDA?

Early childhood care and education workers who are in center-based child care, family child care, or home visitor programs can be evaluated by the Council. These workers need to have some education and experience in early child care and meet several specific requirements:

- Be eighteen years of age or older
- Hold a high school diploma or GED
- Have 480 hours of experience working with young children within the past five years
- Have 120 clock hours of formal child care education within the past five years. It is important to note that the Council will consider waiving certain eligibility requirements if the candidate provides a written explanation, along with documentation that supports the request. Such requests need to be sent to the Council before you submit the CDA application. A Waiver Request form is provided in *The CDA Assessment System and Competency Standards* book in the application packet. The Council will notify the candidate whether the waiver has been granted.

What Kind of Formal Child Care Education Is Needed?

The 120 clock hours of formal child care education must include at least ten hours in each of the following subject areas:

- Planning a safe, healthy environment, including safety, first aid, health, nutrition, space planning, materials and equipment
- Steps to enhance children's physical and intellectual development, for example, large- and small-muscle, language, discovery, art, and music activities
- Positive ways to support children's social and emotional development through self-esteem, independence, self-control, and socialization
- Strategies to establish productive relationships with families through parent or guardian involvement, home visits, conferences, or referrals
- Strategies to manage an effective program operation, including planning, record keeping, and reporting
- Maintaining a commitment to professionalism, for example, through learning about advocacy, ethical practices, workforce issues, or professional associations
- Observing and recording children's behavior, learning tools, and strategies for objective information collection
- Principles of child growth and development, for example, studying developmental milestones from birth through age five or cultural influences on development

The training can be for college credit or for no credit. Formal courses that cover the above topics might have titles such as these:

- Child Growth and Development
- Health, Safety, and Nutrition in Early Childhood Programs
- Guidance Techniques for Early Childhood
- Introduction to the Early Childhood Profession
- Emerging Literacy in Young Children
- Early Childhood Curriculum

You may need to look at a college or agency catalog description for a specific course to see what topics it covers. These hours of training must be obtained from an organization or agency that has expertise in training early childhood teachers, including any of these:

- Four-year colleges and universities
- Two-year junior and community colleges
- Technical and vocational schools
- Resource and referral agencies

- Early childhood education or child care programs that provide training, such as family services, school districts, Head Start, or employer-sponsored in-service trainings
- Programs offered by the state or federal government or by branches of the U.S. military services

Please note that training obtained at conferences or from individual consultants is not accepted by the Council. A candidate may acquire the 120 clock hours of training from one single training program or from a combination of programs. Most CDAs receive their training through credit courses or continuing education units (CEUs). On its website (www.cdacouncil.org), the Council provides the National Directory of Early Childhood Preparation Institutions listed by state to which you can refer.

Is Financial Assistance Available to Help Pay for My Training?

Some state and local organizations offer financial assistance for training, as well as for the CDA assessment fees. For example, some states participate in the Teacher Education and Compensation Helps (T.E.A.C.H.) Early Childhood Project. This program, which originated in North Carolina, provides scholarships for coursework in early childhood education so child care providers can work to increase their compensation. You can visit the Child Care Services Association website at www.childcareservices.org/ps/teach.html to learn more about the T.E.A.C.H. program and to see a listing of participating states. Be sure to inquire through your employer or local early childhood professional association for more information about financial assistance. You may also be able to find free or low-cost training through your local resource and referral agency.

Do I Have to Provide Some Kind of Proof That I Had This Training?

Each agency or organization providing the training must provide proof of your education by means of a letter, certificate, or transcript. Break down the 120 hours into the required subject areas on the Direct Assessment Application form. See appendix A on page 179 for a listing of the CDA subject areas, along with examples of training or course topics that would be covered under each of them.

Are There Different Types of CDA Endorsements?

You may choose from several different CDA endorsements, each in a different setting:

- Center-based infant/toddler
- Center-based preschool
- Family child care
- Home visitor
- Bilingual
- Special education

This choice depends on your specific experience with young children in whichever of the categories you are currently working and where you can be observed functioning as a lead teacher. Although you may not currently hold a lead teacher position at your place of employment, during the advisor's observation, you will need to temporarily assume this role.

You may not choose a setting in which you hope or intend to work in the future. For example, if you are working with infants and toddlers in a center-based program, you may not apply for a Center-Based Preschool Credential because you plan to move into a classroom of older children in the near future. You must first acquire a Center-Based Infant/Toddler Credential because this is the setting in which you currently work and where you will be observed for your CDA. You may, at a later date, work toward a Second Setting Credential for Center-Based Preschool once you have accumulated 480 hours of experience with children in that age group.

What do these settings look like?

Center-based preschool setting This is a state-licensed child development center where a provider works with a group of at least eight children. All of the children in the group are ages three through five years. Also, the entire center-based program needs to have at least ten children enrolled with at least two caregivers working in the center with the children on a regular basis.

Center-based infant/toddler setting This is a licensed child development center where a provider works as a primary caregiver with a group of at least three children ages birth through thirty-six months. Also, the entire center-based program needs to have at least ten children enrolled with at least two caregivers working in the center with the children on a regular basis.

Center-based programs can include nursery schools, child care, Head Start, lab schools, child development programs, or parent cooperatives. They can be full-time or part-time operations and have structured or unstructured schedules. These programs can be in universities, in public schools, churches, or privately owned and operated. Programs that meet the CDA requirements for a center-based setting can be nonprofit or for-profit.

Family child care setting This is a family child care home where a provider works with at least two children, ages five years old or younger. These children are not to be related to the candidate by either blood or marriage. This child care home must meet minimum state and/or local regulations, unless it is located where there is no regulation of family child care.

Home visitor setting This is a program of home visits to families with young children ages birth through five years. Its main focus is providing support and education to parents, helping them meet the needs of their growing children.

Bilingual setting This is a child development center with specific goals for supporting bilingual development in children. In this setting, two languages are consistently used and family involvement is encouraged to attain the program's bilingual goals.

Special education setting This is a child development setting that serves children with moderate to severe special needs. Setting criteria will be the same as for center-based preschool, center-based infant/toddler, or family child care, based on the children's ages and the type of program.

The CDA Process

There are six stages in the CDA process. The first two stages—inquiry and documentation collection—need to be completed before you send in your application to the Council.

1. Inquiry

During this stage, you check the eligibility requirements and make sure you meet them and that you can be observed in an eligible setting. This first stage is also when you decide in which of the settings the assessment will take place (center-based preschool, center-based infant/toddler, or family child care). This choice is based on the setting in which you can be observed in a lead teaching capacity. Remember that you need to choose the setting in which you have your experience and in which you are currently working, *not* a setting in which you plan to work in the future.

When the setting has been determined, you can send away for a packet of application materials. This can be done by contacting the Council for Professional Recognition at 800–424–4310 or ordering online from its website at www.cdacouncil.org. The cost of the application packet as of 2011 is $18, plus shipping and handling. This price is subject to change, so check with the Council

Contact the Council (800–424–4310, www .cdacouncil.org) for more information on the home-visitor setting, bilingual setting, or special education setting.

In any of these settings, a candidate may either be employed or working as a volunteer.

prior to ordering. Tell them which packet you want (center-based preschool, center-based infant/toddler, or family child care). When you receive the application packet, it will contain the following materials:

- Two books outlining the CDA assessment system and the Competency Standards. (These books are different colors, depending on the specific setting. The book for family child care is blue, the center-based preschool book is green, and the center-based infant/toddler book is yellow.)

- A stack of Parent Opinion Questionnaires that you will distribute and have returned to you in sealed envelopes

- Direct Assessment Application form

- CDA Assessment Observation Instrument booklet

As a CDA candidate, you will be assessed on the basis of the Council's national standards. They are the criteria used to evaluate a caregiver's performance with children and families. The Competency Standards are divided into six Competency Goals. Each is a general goal statement for caregiver behavior for any of the settings.

The six Competency Goals are then defined in greater detail by thirteen Functional Areas. These Functional Areas describe more specifically the functions a caregiver must perform to meet the criteria of each Competency Goal and will vary according to a candidate's particular child care setting and/or the age groupings of the children.

These are the six Competency Goals:

Competency Goal I: To establish and maintain a safe, healthy, learning environment

Competency Goal II: To advance physical and intellectual competence

Competency Goal III: To support social and emotional development and to provide positive guidance

Competency Goal IV: To establish positive and productive relationships with families

Competency Goal V: To ensure a well-run, purposeful program responsive to participant needs

Competency Goal VI: To maintain a commitment to professionalism

2. Collection of documentation

During this stage of the process, you begin to assemble your Professional Resource File, which includes a collection of resource materials, an autobiography, and written examples of your competence relating to each of the six CDA Competency Goals. You will also distribute and collect Parent Opinion Questionnaires to determine the parents' opinions of your work with young children.

Also during this second stage, you connect with an advisor. The advisor is the person who observes you at work and who completes the CDA Assessment Observation Instrument.

Often, when a candidate obtains required training through an early childhood education program at a college, university, or training agency, an instructor will also serve as the CDA advisor. If, however, you are not in such a program, it will be up to you to locate a CDA advisor.

You may locate an advisor of your choosing who meets the required criteria, or the Council will provide, upon request, a listing of registered advisors in your particular state. The CDA advisor has to be qualified in these ways:

- Able to relate to people of various ethnic, racial, and socioeconomic backgrounds

- Knowledgeable about national, state, and local requirements and standards for child care programs serving children from birth through five years old

- Familiar with the center where you will be observed (or if you are working in family child care, familiar with family child care) and the needs of the families and children in the community

Additional Requirements

There are additional requirements for the advisor, depending on which type of CDA you are earning. The advisor needs to meet the requirements listed in your *CDA Assessment System and Competency Standards* book in appendix C, Advisor Eligibility Requirements:

Center-Based Preschool

Option 1

- A bachelor of arts, bachelor of science, or advanced degree in early childhood education/child development or home economics/child development from an accredited college or university. The degree must have included twelve semester hours covering the education of children from birth through five years old.

- Two years of experience in a child care setting, serving children from birth through five years old. One year of that time needs to have been spent working directly with children as a caregiver, teacher, child life worker, or social worker, or in a similar role.

- The prospective advisor also needs to have been responsible for the professional growth of another adult for one year.

Option 2

- An associate's or two-year degree in early childhood education/ child development, home economics/child development from an accredited college or university. The degree must have included twelve semester hours covering the education of children from birth through five years old.

- Four years of experience in a child care setting in a program serving children from birth through five years old. Two years of that time needs to have been spent working directly with children as a caregiver, teacher, child life worker, or social worker, or in a similar role.

- The prospective advisor also needs to have been responsible for the professional growth of another adult for two years.

Option 3

- An active CDA Credential.

- Twelve semester hours of study in early childhood education or child development at an accredited college or university, covering children from birth through five years old.

- Six years of experience in a child care setting in a program serving children from birth through five years old. Four years of that time needs to have been spent working directly with children as a caregiver, teacher, child life worker, or social worker, or in a similar role.

- The prospective advisor also needs to have been responsible for the professional growth of another adult for two years.

Center-Based Infant/Toddler

Option 1

- A bachelor of arts, bachelor of science, or advanced degree in early childhood education/child development or in home economics/ child development from an accredited college or university. The degree must have included twelve semester hours covering children from birth through five years old.

- Two years of experience in a child care setting serving children from birth through three years old. One year of that time needs to have been spent working directly with children as a caregiver, teacher, child life worker, or social worker, or in a similar role.

- One year of responsibility for the professional growth of another adult.

Option 2

- An associate's or two-year degree in early childhood education/child development or home economics/child development from an accredited college or university. The degree must have included twelve semester hours covering children from birth through five years old.

- Four years of experience in a child care setting serving children from birth through three years old. Two years of that time needs to have been spent working directly with children as a caregiver, teacher, child life worker, or social worker, or in a similar role.

- Two years of responsibility for the professional growth of another adult.

Option 3

- An active CDA Credential.

- Twelve semester hours of study in early childhood education or child development at an accredited college or university covering children from birth through five years old.

- Six years of experience in a child care setting in a program serving children from birth through three years old, including experience working directly with children as a caregiver, teacher, or child life worker, or in a similar role.

- Two years of responsibility for the professional growth of another adult.

Family Child Care

Option 1

- A bachelor of arts, bachelor of science, or advanced degree in early childhood education/child development or in home economics/child development from an accredited college or university. The degree must have included twelve semester hours covering children from birth through five years old, with two courses on infant/toddler development.

- Two years of experience in a child care setting serving children from birth through five years old. One year of that time needs to have been spent working directly with children in the same age range as the children in your home, as a caregiver, teacher, child life worker, or social worker, or in a similar role.

- The prospective advisor also needs to have been responsible for the professional growth of another adult for one year or have held a leadership position in a child care organization.

- Experience in a family child care setting as a provider, trainer, or parent.

Option 2

- An associate's or two-year degree in early childhood education/child development or home economics/child development from an accredited college or university. The degree must have included twelve semester hours covering children from birth through five years old, with two courses on infant/toddler development.

- Four years of experience in a child care setting in a program serving children from birth through five years old, including experience working directly with children in the same age range as the children in your home, as a caregiver, teacher, child life worker, or social worker, or in a similar role.

- The prospective advisor also needs to have been responsible for the professional growth of another adult or have held a leadership position in a child care organization.

Option 3

- An active CDA Credential.

- Twelve semester hours of study in early childhood education or child development at an accredited college or university covering children from birth through five years old.

- Six years of experience in a child care setting in a program serving children from birth through five years old, including experience working directly with children in the same age range as the children in your home, as a caregiver, teacher, child life worker, or social worker, or in a similar role.

- The prospective advisor also needs to have been responsible for the professional growth of another adult or have held a leadership position in a child care organization.

Keep in mind that your choice of an advisor could present a conflict of interest. For the advisor to conduct an objective and credible assessment observation, you need to choose someone who meets certain additional requirements:

- The advisor must not be working as a co-teacher with you on a daily basis with the same group of children.

- The advisor must not be a relative of a child in your care at any time during the assessment process.

- The advisor must not be related by blood or marriage or other legal relationship to you.

Having a good CDA advisor is important. If at all possible, locate an advisor who will agree to spend some time with you during the CDA process, rather than merely conducting the final assessment observation. Ideally, the advisor you choose will be your mentor. She will be there to answer your questions, look over your Professional Resource File, proofread your Competency Goal Statements and autobiography, give you valuable tips, help prepare your setting so it meets Council standards, and intercede for you, if necessary.

Your advisor is the person in your corner, your cheerleader throughout this process. She should take the job seriously and consider your success in getting a CDA Credential her responsibility and a direct reflection on herself. If you feel your advisor is anything less, look for another!

3. Application

If you work in a center, you, your advisor, and your center director will fill out the Direct Assessment Application form. This application form will be sent to the Council, along with documentation of the 120 hours of training, and the application fee, which is $325 as of 2011. This fee may change so be sure to check in your application packet for any updates. The Council for Professional Recognition is developing an online application process. See pages 14–15 for more information.

After you send in your application to the Council, three stages in the CDA process remain to be completed.

4. Verification visit by the Council representative

After the Council receives the completed application form and verifies your eligibility, it will assign a specially trained early childhood professional to meet with you. This Council representative will call to set up an appointment for a verification visit.

The meeting place can be decided between you and the Council representative. If you are in a center-based program, the verification visit can be, but does not have to be, conducted in your place of employment. A quiet place is preferable, such as a public library or somewhere on a college campus where a private room with a door and adult chairs and tables are available. If you are a family child care provider, the verification visit may not be conducted in your home or in any other private home.

During this meeting, the Council representative will give you a written, sixty-question, multiple-choice exam called the Early

You will need to have your Professional Resource File completed before the Council representative's visit.

Childhood Studies Review. This test measures your knowledge of good practices in early childhood education. Your performance on this exam is only one part of the documentation that the Council considers in its decision to award the CDA Credential. You will not receive your grade for this exam.

The Council representative will also give you an oral interview. During this interview, you should demonstrate your expertise in several early childhood situations. Additionally, the representative will check your Professional Resource File to see whether it is accurate and complete.

At the conclusion of the visit, the representative will collect several things from you:

- The CDA Assessment Observation Instrument booklet that your advisor completed, which must be in a sealed envelope

- The completed Parent Opinion Questionnaires, also in a sealed envelope

- Copies of your Competency Goals and Competency Goal Statements (the six essays)

- A copy of your autobiography

The documentation items must be prepared/collected/compiled *within six months* of submitting the application form. All of these items, along with your answer sheet from the Early Childhood Studies Review and the results of the oral interview, will be sent by the Council representative to the Council in Washington, DC, where they will be evaluated.

The Council schedules verification visits within ninety days of receiving a completed application form. Before preparing the documentation items as listed above, you should decide when you want to have a verification visit scheduled and then be sure to submit the application form accordingly.

CDA online application and assessment

The Council for Professional Recognition is developing an online application and assessment process, which will be available as an option to CDA candidates. The traditional paper application and assessment procedures will still be available.

The online process will enable candidates to establish a login name and password to begin their application. The application form will be completed online, and the verification of training and experience will be transmitted electronically. If the candidate is working in a center-based program, the center director will also establish a login name and password so needed information can be submitted. The candidate's CDA advisor will have a similar login name and password. The process will move forward as each party submits the information requested. If one party fails to submit information, the process will stop until it is completed. All parties will be able to see the progression of the application process online. Just like the traditional paper application process, the online process will have no application deadlines to meet. Verification visits will be scheduled within ninety days of the submission of complete and correct application documentation by the candidate, the advisor, and the candidate's employer, if applicable.

At first, only the application process will be available online. Eventually, CDA candidates may be able to complete the Early Childhood Studies Review and respond to the oral interview scenarios online as well. The Council is still focused on ensuring the competency of those applying for the Credential. The new online process will not be an "easy way out" of the application process. Candidates will still be observed by an advisor, assemble a Professional Resource File, collect Parent Questionnaires, and compose the six Competency Goal Statements. Updates about this new online system will be announced on the Council's website. Candidates can also subscribe to the Council's electronic newsletter, *CouncilLink*, on the website or by sending an e-mail to newsletter@cdacouncil.org.

5. Credential award

A Council committee looks over the materials sent to them by the Council representative. Because quite a few components compose the CDA assessment—including the acquired training, Early Childhood Studies Review exam, assessment observation, oral interview, Professional Resource File, Competency Goal Statements, and other items—the committee's decision is not based on only one component but on all of these components taken as a whole. If everything meets with the Council's approval, the credential is awarded and is sent to the new CDA.

If the Council committee determines, for one reason or another, that you do not qualify for a credential, you will be notified and informed of appeal procedures and other options of what to do next. All information about CDA candidates is confidential. The Council will not release assessment information to anyone without your permission.

6. *Credential renewal*

A CDA Credential is valid for three years. After that, you may renew it for five-year periods. To do that you will need to order a renewal packet. This can be ordered from the Council for $13, plus shipping and handling. This price may be subject to change, so please check with the Council prior to ordering. A CDA may renew her credential only for the original setting, age-level endorsement, and specialization.

The following chapters include step-by-step instructions for assembling your Professional Resource File and writing the Competency Goal Statements. You will learn how to prepare for the assessment observation by your CDA advisor and the verification visit with the CDA representative. You will find the help you need, specific to your particular age-level endorsement and setting, in chapter 3 for center-based preschool, chapter 4 for center-based infant/toddler, or chapter 5 for family child care.

Preparing for
the CDA Process

2

Organizing the Professional Resource File

The Professional Resource File is your portfolio of work. When complete, it will show all of the components required by the Council for your type of endorsement. This chapter reviews the components required of all applicants. After you become familiar with the components, you will read the next chapter in this book—either chapter 3, 4, or 5—that pertains to your specific endorsement.

Putting together your Professional Resource File can be relatively easy if you are organized. The Council doesn't really care how the file is put together, as long as it is complete and legible. For example, it can be bound in a binder or contained inside folders in a file box. Either way, items can easily be added or deleted.

I suggest a two-inch, loose-leaf, three-ring binder. Get one that has a clear-plastic sleeve on the front so you can slip in a cover sheet with the title "Professional Resource File" and your name. The advantage of the binder over the file box is its portability—it's rather inconvenient to carry around a file box. Also, it's much easier to look through a binder, because everything is bound inside rather than sliding around in file folders. To make your binder attractive, well-organized, and easy for the Council representative to evaluate, this chapter will offer some specific suggestions for setting it up.

Have your *CDA Assessment System and Competency Standards* book handy, which the Council sent in your application packet. The book will be green for center-based preschool care, yellow for center-based infant/toddler care, or blue for family child care. If you are borrowing one of these books from a friend who has already earned their CDA Credential, make sure the book has a copyright date no earlier than 2006. Effective September 1, 2011, the Professional Resource File must be consistent with the requirements outlined in Competency Standards books dated 2006 or later. Refer to the book as you read the following suggestions for compiling your file. The Council provides you with two of these books as part of the application packet, one for you to keep and one for you to give to your advisor.

Look in your CDA book at the Professional Resource Collection section in part 2. The seventeen resources you need to collect are listed there under their applicable Competency Goals:

Competency Goal I: Items 1–4

Competency Goal II: Items 5–6

Competency Goal III: Items 7–9

Competency Goal IV: Items 10–11

Competency Goal V: Item 12

Competency Goal VI: Items 13–17

To get your binder ready, you will need a pack of at least twenty-five clear plastic page protectors and a pack of at least eight dividers with tabs. Also, you will want to get a pack of self-stick, plain white labels (1-inch by 3-inch is a good size).

Put the dividers in the binder first, making small labels to stick on the eight side tabs as follows:

1. Autobiography

2. Competency Goal I

3. Competency Goal II

4. Competency Goal III

5. Competency Goal IV

6. Competency Goal V

7. Competency Goal VI

8. Competency Goal Statements

Sections 2–7 will contain the seventeen items of your Professional Resource Collection. Section 8 will contain your six Competency Goal Statements.

Writing the Autobiography

This essay needs to be about 300 words long. You may be thinking, "How can I possibly come up with 300 words about myself?" Once you begin writing, however, you will probably find it hard to limit yourself to only 300 words! It is to be written in the first person: "I became interested in teaching...."

The autobiography consists of two main parts:

1. A brief overview of your life so far...who you are! You will mention a few important events in your life that made a difference in where you find yourself today. Be careful to avoid information that is too personal or may not be appropriate in the Professional Resource File. For example, it would not be prudent to include information about a troubled family life or series of divorces. Write instead about the positive experiences you have had and relate those in your essay.

2. A description of what or who in your life influenced your decision to work with young children, for example, such influences as working at a summer camp, taking care of siblings, or the babysitting jobs you had as a teenager.

You may write the autobiography as you like, but the above two items must be included. The Council committee members who review your materials will be looking for those items specifically. It is a good idea to end the autobiography on a positive, forward-looking note. You can include a projection of your personal goals for your future in the early childhood profession, in both the short and long term. These may be educational goals, such as courses or degrees, and/or career goals, such as becoming a lead teacher, a center director, or perhaps the owner of a child care center.

Use an easy-to-read font, such as Times New Roman or Arial, in a 12-point size to type your autobiography and all other items for the Professional Resource File. Please be sure to use your software's spell-checking and grammar-checking functions before printing your final copy, because you may not catch all errors when reading over your paper. You are presenting yourself as a professional and your writing should reflect this.

Before you punch holes in your autobiography and put it into your Professional Resource File binder, make a copy of it. You will give the copy to the Council representative at the verification visit. This is one of several documents you will need to give to the representative, so begin compiling those in a separate pocket folder.

Behind the first divider in your file, which is tabbed "Auto-biography," put one empty page protector. Into this you will insert the autobiography you have just written. The pages of this document can be placed back to back in the page protector. If you have not completed your autobiography, this page protector will make a good placeholder. You may also want to include a current résumé behind your autobiography (optional), in which case you would need yet another page protector. Your binder is now ready for the seventeen required resources, as outlined in your CDA book. These will be placed in the sections 2–7, tabbed Competency Goals I–VI.

Distributing and Collecting the Parent Opinion Questionnaires

How parents view the CDA candidate, in terms of knowledge and skill, is very important. Parents who have a child in your classroom will fill out a Parent Opinion Questionnaire. A stack of questionnaires are included in the CDA application packet. No one (including you) other than officials authorized by the Council is permitted to read them. When deciding when to distribute these questionnaires, remember that they must be dated and collected within six months prior to the time the Direct Assessment Application form is submitted.

You need to fill out the cover page, indicating your name, the date the questionnaire should be returned, and a telephone number where you can be reached. The questionnaire is in English and Spanish. If a parent or guardian speaks a language other than English or Spanish, try to find someone to translate the questions. If the family members require any extra help filling out the form, someone other than you needs to supply the help, for confidentiality reasons.

To start the process, contact each family in person or by phone, explain a little bit about the CDA Credential, why you are interested in earning one, and the importance of obtaining the Parent Opinion Questionnaires from each of the families in your program. You may also distribute these questionnaires at a group meeting or mail them to families, along with self-addressed, stamped envelopes. Only one questionnaire will be filled out per family. The Council requires that you collect enough completed forms to equal at least 75 percent of the total number of Parent Opinion Questionnaires distributed.

Distribute each Parent Opinion Questionnaire with a plain envelope so the family can return the completed form in the envelope with the flap sealed. When all of the envelopes have been returned, place them unopened in a large envelope and seal it. Write your name on the front of this envelope, along with the number of questionnaires distributed and the number returned. The result should look like this:

Parent Opinion Questionnaires
Mary Smith
10 out of 12

You'll give this sealed envelope of Parent Opinion Questionnaires to the Council representative during the verification visit.

All you have left to do is create a title sheet to slide under the transparent sleeve on the front cover of your binder. This will be typed in a large, bold font, centered on the page. It will read as follows:

Mary Smith
Professional Resource File
Date

Leave the date blank for now, because this will be the date of your verification visit. You can add the date later, when your verification visit is scheduled. Resist the temptation to decorate the title sheet with clip art, drawings, or photos. You can put a narrow border around the outside, but remember this is a Professional Resource File and, as such, should look neat, sharp, and *professional*. After the verification visit, you can personalize your file any way you like.

CDA Process: Center-Based Preschool

YOUR DECISION TO TEACH PRESCHOOL CHILDREN is an important one. These early years are when children develop first friendships, establish a good sense of self-esteem, gain a basic understanding of the world around them, and learn to be independent. As their teacher, you are responsible for providing a developmentally appropriate environment and experiences that will form a strong foundation for their future development and success in school. This is not a responsibility to be taken lightly, because it is your skill and effectiveness in the classroom that ultimately determine the quality of the entire program.

In recent years, the number of three- to five-year-old children who are in group programs has increased significantly. This is due to the corresponding increase in prekindergartens, public preschools, kindergartens, Head Start programs, child care, and other publicly or privately funded settings. As a preschool caregiver, you are a special person in the lives of the children you teach, as they form first friendships, learn new skills, gain independence, and advance their understanding of themselves and the world. Working with preschool children also involves close relationships with the families, since they represent the children's first and most important teachers. By promoting collaboration during these early years, preschool caregivers are setting a precedent for family participation throughout these children's school years.

The CDA Competency Standards outline the skills that preschool care providers need to meet the unique needs of three-, four-, and five-year-old children. *The Child Development Associate Assessment System and Competency Standards for Preschool Caregivers in Center-Based Programs* (Council for Professional Recognition 2011) was recently revised to include the following:

- Restructured Competency Standards that reflect current research about supporting preschool children's development in early childhood centers
- Updated concepts and terminology
- Principles for supporting infants and toddlers who are dual-language learners

To gain or retain a position in a quality child development center, expect advancement, and seek proper compensation, you are pursuing a CDA Credential and are becoming an early childhood professional. As such, you will need to demonstrate your competency in meeting the needs of preschool children. Having nearly completed or completed the 120 clock hours of training, you are ready to begin the CDA process. Your Professional Resource File should now be set up and ready to fill with the Professional Resource Collection.

Assembling the Professional Resource Collection

You have already completed your autobiography, and it should be in the first section of your Professional Resource File. Next, type a label for the second divider page, whose tab you labeled "Competency Goal I." Type the label as follows:

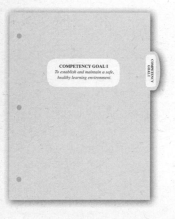

COMPETENCY GOAL I
*To establish and maintain a safe,
healthy learning environment*

Looking in your green book, you will see this written in bold print on page 17. Notice that the first line is capitalized and the second line is italicized. You will do the same. Place the label in the center of the second divider page, whose tab you labeled "Competency Goal I." Behind this second divider, insert four empty page protectors.

Now type a label to place on each of these page protectors. On the labels, type the numbered items listed under Competency Goal I. On the first label, for example, type the following, being sure to include the number:

> **1. Provide a summary of the legal requirements in your state regarding child abuse and neglect (including contact information for the appropriate agency) and also your program's policy regarding your responsibility to report child abuse and neglect.**

Place the label on the upper right-hand corner of the first empty page protector. You now know instantly what goes into that page protector. You can probably find this information in your state child care licensing regulations or from your state child abuse prevention agency. Remember to include the phone number to call for information or to report abuse. Also, find out what the policy for reporting child abuse is for your particular child care center. Type this up after the previous information, under a heading, such as "My Program's Policies for Reporting Child Abuse." Print all of this and insert it into the first page protector. Make sure to position the information on the paper so the label on the page protector isn't covering it.

Even when you have put all the resources into the page protectors, keep the labels on them, as it makes the CDA representative's job much easier. She can see, without a doubt, that all seventeen items are there and that your file is complete.

The second page protector in this section will have a label typed as follows:

> **2. Include the current certificate of completion of a certified pediatric first-aid training course (that includes treatment for blocked airway and providing rescue breathing for infants and young children). Certification must have been within the past three years.**

Now place this label on the top right corner of the second page protector. Make a photocopy of your first-aid certificate and insert it into this page protector.

The third page protector in this section will have a label typed as follows:

> **3. Use the Internet, the public library, or your program's professional library to obtain the name and contact information for an agency that supplies information on nutrition for children and/or nutrition education for families.**

Make sure your training was for pediatric first aid, *not* adult first aid! Do not include a copy of your CPR certificate unless it is combined with your first-aid certificate. It was not requested and the Council frowns on items being included in the Professional Resource File that were not asked for specifically.

You do not need to put the italicized words you see in parentheses (for example, *Cooperative Extension Service or Child Care Food Program*) on the label.

Place this label on the third page protector. After you locate the requested information, type it, print it, and insert it into this page protector. The fourth page protector in this section will have a label typed as follows:

> **4. Provide a sample of your weekly plan that includes goals for children's learning and development, brief descriptions of planned learning experiences, and also accommodations for children with special needs (whether for children you currently serve or may serve in the future).**

You can use the weekly activity plan form you usually use in your program, perhaps enlarging it to accommodate the information that is required. Be sure to address all of the typical learning areas, such as art, language/literacy, circle, fine/gross motor, dramatic play, math, and science. In addition to listing the activities, you need to write learning goals for each activity, that is, what you expect the children to learn or how their development will be enhanced by doing the activity. You must also explain how each of your activities could be adapted to enable a child with special needs to participate. For an example of this, see the sample Weekly Activity Plan for Preschoolers provided on page 189. You have now completed collecting resources for Competency Goal I and are ready to move on to Competency Goal II. Make a label for the third divider page, whose tab you have labeled "Competency Goal II." This label should read as follows:

> **COMPETENCY GOAL II**
> *To advance physical and intellectual competence*

Place the label in the center of the divider page. Then place four page protectors behind this divider. Only the first page protector needs to be labeled. Here's how the label on the first page protector should read:

> **5. Select four songs, fingerplays, word games, or poems that you can use to promote phonological awareness. Describe strategies to promote phonological awareness among children whose home language is other than English.**

Place this label on the top right corner of the first page protector. You can go to the library and look in the children's department to find what you need. Ask the children's librarian to show you books that promote phonological awareness. You can also search the Internet for these items.

Phonological awareness means hearing the sounds of letters and words. For young children, choosing songs, word games, and poems with an abundance of rhyming words and/or alliteration will help them in this area. *Alliteration* means the repetition of the same or similar consonant sounds at the beginning of words, as in "The tiny tiger took a tumble." Children whose home language is not English will benefit from similar activities, but teachers can also include activities in their native languages.

You can either type the items yourself or print examples from the Internet. Your explanation of strategies for promoting phonological awareness with English-language learners (ELL) should be typed on a separate page. Put these pages in the four page protectors, back to back.

Now, make a label for the next resource item you will put in your file, typing it as follows:

> **6. Describe nine learning experiences for 3-, 4-, and 5-year-old children (three for 3-year-olds, three for 4-year-olds, and three for 5-year-olds). Each learning experience should promote physical, cognitive, and creative development. Describe the goals, materials, and teaching strategies used.**

Add three more page protectors to this section, placing the label you have just made in the upper right corner of the first one.

Describe the nine activities, three for each age group. For each activity, provide a title, a list of goals (what you want the children to do or learn), a list of materials needed, and the procedure for presenting the activity to children (step by step). Then explain how the activity promotes physical, cognitive, and creative development. It should look something like the following example:

Activity for Three-Year-Olds

example

Title: Basketball

Goal: Children will roll a ball toward a target on the floor.

Materials: Round, plastic laundry basket, inflated beach ball, and masking tape

Procedure: Set laundry basket on its side on the floor. About five feet from the open end of the basket, stick a length of masking tape on the floor. Have the children take turns standing behind the tape line to roll the ball

This example is provided solely for demonstration purposes, to suggest the format and the type of content required. It should *not* be used in your Professional Resource File. You need to provide examples of activities you actually use in your program with preschool children.

into the open basket. The tape line can be backed up as the children become skilled with the activity. The teacher will demonstrate the activity beforehand and provide encouragement as the children participate.

This is a physical activity because it enhances large-motor development and coordination as the children push the ball toward the basket.

This is a cognitive activity because the children stand behind a tape line and decide how hard to push the ball toward the basket.

This is a creative activity because the children move the ball any way they like toward the basket, such as with hands or feet or by standing up or kneeling down.

Describe two more activities for three-year-olds, using this format. Next, using the same format, describe three activities appropriate for four-year-olds. Finally, describe three activities appropriate for five-year-olds. You will have a total of nine activities. Type the three activities for each age group on separate pages. Place the pages back to back in the page protectors.

You are now finished collecting resources for Competency Goal II and are ready to move on to Competency Goal III. Make a label for the fourth divider page, whose tab you have labeled "Competency Goal III." This label should read as follows:

> **COMPETENCY GOAL III**
> *To support social and emotional development*
> *and to provide positive guidance*

Place the label in the center of the divider page. Then place three page protectors behind this divider. The label for the first page protector should read like this:

> **7. Provide the titles, authors, publishers, copyright dates, and a short summary for each of ten age-appropriate children's books *that you use* to support development of children's self-concept and self-esteem and to help children deal with life's challenges.**

Place this label on the first page protector. Go to the library and ask the children's librarian to help you find these books. Be sure to choose books that have copyright dates less than ten years old.

Books that help children deal with life challenges, such as death, moving to a new home, starting a new school, or welcoming a new baby, are known as *bibliotherapy* or *therapeutic* books. Do *not* cut and paste information from an Internet bookstore. These are to be books you have actually used with the children in your program and with which you are very familiar. Type the information requested on one or two pages and insert them back to back in the first page protector.

Next, type a label for the second page protector as follows:

> **8. Use the Internet, the public library, or your program's professional library to obtain at least two resources designed to assist teachers in constructively dealing with children with challenging behaviors (such as aggressive behavior like hitting or biting, or shyness).**

Place this label on the second page protector. Again, the librarian at your local library will be able to help you find the books and information you need. These will not be children's materials; they will be books or articles for *teachers*. Be sure to list at least two resources. Type the information and insert it into this page protector.

The third page protector should be labeled as follows:

> **9. Provide the name and telephone number of an agency in the community where you work for making referrals to family counseling.**

Be sure the agency you select is located in the community where you work and not merely a website or an agency somewhere in your state. Type the information and insert it into this page protector. You are now finished collecting resources for Competency Goal III and are ready to move on to Competency Goal IV.

In the center of the fifth divider, whose tab you labeled "Competency Goal IV," place a label that reads like this:

> **COMPETENCY GOAL IV**
> *To establish positive and productive relationships with families*

Behind this divider page, put two page protectors. Label the first page protector as follows:

> **10. Find out where to obtain resources, materials, and translation services for families whose home language is other than English. Provide the agency name and contact information.**

Locate the name of the local agency, along with its address and phone number. Find the name(s) of someone at the agency to contact for information. Type this information and insert it into this page protector.

The second page protector should be labeled as follows:

> **11. Document your program's policies that specify parents' responsibilities and what the program does for parents.**

You may find this information in your center's parent handbook or orientation materials. It may be helpful to format the information this way:

example

What My Program Does for Parents

- Provides their children with a warm, loving, and safe place to play and learn

- Provides their children with nutritious snacks and meals

- Provides their children with trained and qualified caregivers

- Provides parent or guardian meetings in which the adults can gain information about a variety of parenting topics and get acquainted with other families

What Parents Can Do for My Program

- Respect the center's illness policy

- Pick up their children on time

- Provide a complete change of clothing at the center in case of accidents

- Visit the classroom and participate with their child or children whenever possible

Remember, these are provided only as examples. You must use your own center's policies, specific to your program!

You are now finished collecting resources for Competency Goal IV and are ready to move on to Competency Goal V.

In the center of the sixth divider, whose tab you labeled "Competency Goal V," place this label:

Behind this divider, place three page protectors. Type a label that reads as follows to place on the first one.

> **12. Provide three samples of record-keeping forms used in early childhood programs. Include an accident report, an emergency form, and a third form of your choice.**

Be sure to include the two types of forms that are specifically requested: the accident report and the emergency form. The third form could be a registration form, an attendance sign-in sheet, a field-trip permission form, or a daily report form. Put each requested form in the page protectors. You have now completed the resource collection for Competency Goal V and are ready to move on to Competency Goal VI.

In the center of the seventh divider, whose tab you labeled "Competency Goal VI," place a label that reads like this:

> **COMPETENCY GOAL VI**
>
> *To maintain a commitment to professionalism*

Behind this divider, place several page protectors. Type a label that reads as follows to place on the first one.

> **13. Use the Internet, the public library, or your program's professional library to obtain the name, address, and phone number of your state's agency that regulates child care centers and homes. Describe two important requirements related to your job responsibilities.**

Type only the name, address, and phone number of your state's child care regulating agency and place this page in the first page protector. Then go to the website listed below to look up the child care regulations for your particular state:

National Resource Center of Health and Safety in Child Care
http://nrckids.org/STATES/states.htm

Print out the section(s) that describes the qualification requirements for personnel (teachers, directors, and assistants). You can find this information in the regulations under "Staffing,"

"Personnel Policies," or something similar. Print only these particular sections for your file. In these sections, locate a listing of important requirements that are related to your own particular job responsibilities as a teacher, an assistant teacher, or a director and highlight them with a yellow highlighting marker. Now, put these regulations in page protectors.

Choose two of the highlighted requirements and type them on a separate page with this title: "Requirements Related to My Job Responsibilities." Put this in the first labeled page protector, in front of the regulations.

Type a label for the next page protector that reads as follows:

> **14. Review the websites of two or three national early childhood associations (one with a local affiliate) to obtain information about membership, their resources, and how to order. Download at least two resources from the Internet that will enhance your work.**

These associations could include the National Association for the Education of Young Children (NAEYC, www.naeyc.org) or the National Association of Child Care Professionals (NACCP, www.naccp.org). Type the requested information about the two or three associations, and place it in the page protector. Be sure to include information about becoming a member, the types of resources that are available for download or purchase from each website, and how a person can order them.

Now find two articles on one of the websites that relate to your work with preschoolers. On the NAEYC website (www.naeyc.org), you can access back issues of *Young Children*, which has many articles from which to choose. Print two articles and put them back to back in page protectors.

The next page protector will be labeled as follows:

> **15. Obtain four pamphlets or articles designed to help parents understand how young children develop and learn. Articles must help parents understand development and learning of 3- to 5-year-olds. At least one article must relate to guidance.**

Put each pamphlet or article in its own page protector. Only the first page protector needs to be labeled. You can find some pamphlets like this at a pediatrician's office, your local hospital, the health department, or perhaps the public library. Articles may also be downloaded from the Internet. Be sure the pamphlets or articles you choose are written primarily for parents and guardians and address topics about how children grow and learn during the preschool years. This could include information about stages of development and what to expect a child to be doing at specific ages. It would *not* include information about immunizations, dental or physical health, or safety. Do not include items about infants, toddlers, or school-age children. Remember that one of the pamphlets or articles has to be about guidance and that you have been asked to include four items. Do *not* include more or less than four!

The next page protector will be labeled as follows:

> **16. Locate an observation tool to use in recording information about children's behavior. One copy should be blank; the other one should be filled out as a sample of your observation of an individual child.**

Use a form you typically use in your work with preschool children. If you do not have such a form, you can use the observation tool provided in appendix B on page 181. It is for recording an anecdotal record. An anecdotal record is a type of observation tool. It is a short, written record based on observation of a child's behavior. You may put both copies (one blank and one filled out) back to back in the same page protector. *Do not include the child's name on the observation.*

The next page protector will be labeled as follows:

> **17. Obtain contact information for at least two agencies in the community that provide resources and services for children with disabilities.**

Find information on two or three agencies, which might include those that provide physical therapy, occupational therapy, speech therapy, or other developmental or learning services. In some communities, the local school district provides these services. Be sure these are local agencies that families enrolled in your program can access. Include the name of each agency, its address, its phone number, and names of a person(s) who can be contacted for information. Type this information and insert it into this page protector.

If all of your page protectors are filled, the Professional Resource Collection section of your Professional Resource File is complete! Resist the temptation to add materials and information that were not specifically asked for in your green book. This will not impress the Council representative. On the contrary, it will indicate your inability to follow instructions and may interfere with the representative's ability to sort through the resources to determine whether your file is complete.

That being said, this Professional Resource File does belong to you. The Council representative will look it over and check it for accuracy but will not keep it. The Professional Resource Collection will be a valuable source of reference to you as a professional. After you receive your CDA Credential, you can continue to add resources to the original collection for your own personal use.

You are now ready to work on the third and final portion of the Professional Resource File: Competency Goal Statements. This is the last tabbed section of your file.

Writing the Competency Goal Statements

The national Competency Standards are used to evaluate a CDA candidate's skills in working with young children. Six Competency Goals within these standards state general goals for caregiver performance. Under each of the Competency Goals are one or more Functional Areas, for a total of thirteen. The thirteen Functional Areas define more specifically the skills and behaviors you must perform to meet each of the Competency Goals.

Your task is to rewrite, in *your own* words and with *your own* individual understanding, each of the thirteen Functional Area statements. Next, you will provide several very specific examples from your own work with young children, which will demonstrate your competency in each of those Functional Areas.

Refer to pages 37–78 in your green CDA book. There you will see the Competency Goals written with the Functional Area statements in the green boxes beneath them. Below that, each Functional Area is further defined by a Developmental Context or explanation. Finally, you will see a listing of examples of caregiver competence for each of the Functional Areas.

Look at pages 39–47 in your CDA book to find Competency Goal I. Notice that it has three Functional Areas: Safe, Healthy, and Learning Environment. Begin writing your first Competency Goal Statement by typing what you see written, with the first line in bold print and the second line in italics:

Competency Goal I
To establish and maintain a safe, healthy learning environment

Functional Area 1: Safe

Now, instead of writing what you see in the green box in your book, you will need to rewrite it in your own words. Instead of writing "Candidate provides a safe environment and teaches children safe practices to prevent and reduce injuries," you will personalize this statement in your own words. For some ideas on doing this, read the Developmental Context section under the Functional Area on page 39 in the green book. Two examples of what you might write are

> I make sure to provide a setting that promotes safety and minimizes the risk of injuries.

example

> Safety is a main priority in the environment I provide for the children in my care. I make every effort to prevent injuries and accidents.

example

You can see that I've included all the main ideas of the Council's version but in my own words. Now write *your own* version. Do not use the word *will* in the statement, because this is not something you *will* be doing, but rather something you are doing right now. So, if this were *my* Competency Goal Statement, it would look like this so far:

Competency Goal I
To establish and maintain a safe, healthy learning environment

example

Functional Area 1: Safe
Safety is a main priority in the environment that I provide for the children in my care. I make every effort to prevent injuries and accidents.

You will now give *specific* examples of things *you* do in *your* program to satisfy this goal. If you look in your green book, you will see a list of examples on pages 39–41. You may *not* copy these examples. They are meant to give you ideas. Also, they are much too general in nature. You should write examples that are specific to your own work with young children in your program. For instance, one of the examples given in the book on page 40 reads, "Supervises all children's activities indoors and outdoors." I may supervise the children in *my* program too, but what do I do specifically? After thinking about it, I would write something like this:

> I do this by positioning myself in the classroom and on the playground so that all areas of the room are visible to me. I make a point of moving around, so I can oversee the children's activities and interact with them.

example

Continue to write two or three more specific examples under this Functional Area 1: Safe. You can write them as a bulleted list or in a descriptive paragraph. If I chose to write the examples in a bulleted list, my completed statement for Functional Area 1: Safe would look like this:

Competency Goal I
To establish an d maintain a safe, healthy learning environment

Functional Area 1: Safe

Safety is a main priority in the environment that I provide for the children in my care. I make every effort to prevent injuries and accidents.

I do this by

- Positioning myself in the classroom and on the playground so that all areas of the room are visible to me. I make a point of moving around, so I can oversee the children's activities and interact with them.

- *(Another example).*

- *(Another example).*

When you finish writing *your* examples, you can begin your Competency Goal Statement for Functional Area 2. Leave a few spaces and write this:

Functional Area 2: Healthy

On page 42 in your book, look at the statement written in the green box. It reads, "Candidate provides an environment that promotes health and prevents illness and teaches children about good nutrition and practices that promote wellness." Rewrite it in *your own* words, looking at the Developmental Context on page 42 for ideas. I might write something like this:

I encourage proper nutrition and good health habits every day by modeling these behaviors and providing an environment that promotes them and where risk of illness is reduced.

You try writing it in *your own* words. After you do, type "I do this by."

You may now give some specific examples of things you do in your program to satisfy this goal. Do *not* copy the examples provided in your book, but do gain some ideas from them. One of these examples on page 43 in the book reads, "Makes sure play areas and materials are cleaned daily." So, I might write this:

At the end of each day, I wash all toys that have been handled by the children in warm, soapy water. Those items that cannot be washed in the sink are sanitized with a safe, nontoxic spray and left to air-dry.

You will need to write two or three of *your own* specific examples under Functional Area 2: Healthy. Use the format suggested previously.

When you finish your examples, you are ready to begin your Competency Goal Statement for Functional Area 3. Leave a few spaces and write this:

Functional Area 3: Learning Environment

Look at the statement written in the green box on page 45 in your book. It reads, "Candidate organizes and uses relationships, the physical space, materials, the daily schedule, and routines to create a secure, interesting, and enjoyable environment that promotes engagement, play, exploration, and learning of all children, including children with disabilities and special needs." Rewrite it in *your own* words, looking at the Developmental Context on page 45 for ideas. I might write something like this:

> The learning environment I provide encourages children to feel comfortable, to be curious, to explore, and to learn. This is done through interesting activities, materials, and opportunities for socialization.

example

You try writing it in *your own* words. After you do, type "I do this by."

Now you are ready to write *specific* examples of how *you* satisfy this goal in *your* program. Look at the samples given in the book on pages 45–47, using them for ideas. You will need to write three examples. Here is a sample of a specific example:

> I put all the children's toys in open bins that are labeled with pictures. They are stored on low, open shelves so the children have easy access to them and quickly learn how to put the toys away themselves.

example

After writing your three examples for this Functional Area, you will be finished with Competency Goal I.

The writing you have done for this Competency Goal must add up to between 200 and 500 words. Count only the words in the Functional Area statements and the examples under each of them, not the words you copied from the green-tinted boxes. Please be sure to do a word count on your computer to be certain you are within this word-count range, as the Council is very particular about this. It is better to be closer to 500 words, because a thorough explanation of your competency is better than one that is too short and incomplete. That said, you should not go over 500 words, because the Council sees that as a failure to follow instructions and you will lose points. If your word count is well under 500 words, add additional examples under the Functional Areas. If you have more than 500 words, take out a couple of your examples.

Now you are ready to go on to Competency Goal II. Find it in your book on page 48. You will see that this Competency Goal has four Functional Areas: Physical, Cognitive, Communication, and Creative.

Begin Competency Goal II on a new page by copying what you see written, with the first line in bold print and the second line in italics:

Competency Goal II
To advance physical and intellectual competence

Functional Area 4: Physical

Now, rewrite what you see in the green box. It should be in *your own* words. Read the Developmental Context on page 48 for ideas. I might write something like this:

example

> In my program, children have daily opportunities, both indoors and outdoors, to participate in activities that enhance their physical development.

You try writing it in *your own* words. Then type "I do this by."

Now give three specific examples of how *you* meet this goal in *your* program. Think of specific examples that may involve small- or large-motor development. Look at the examples on pages 48–50 for ideas, but do *not* copy them. Here is a sample of a specific example:

example

> Setting up a different obstacle course every Wednesday with equipment the children enjoy. I use tunnels, balance beams, tumbling mats, and small climbers.

You can see that this example is very specific. Make sure yours are too!

When you have finished writing your three examples, you are ready to go on to Functional Area 5. Find Functional Area 5 on page 51 in your book. Leave a few spaces and type this heading:

Functional Area 5: Cognitive

Look at the statement in the green box. Write that statement in your own words. Read the Developmental Context on page 51 for ideas. I might write something like this:

example

> I feel it is important for children to exercise their curiosity and have opportunities to problem solve, so I provide an

environment and activities that allow for discovery and exploration.

Now, you write it in *your own* words. Then type "I do this by." Write three examples of how *you* satisfy this goal in *your* program. Look at the samples given in your book for ideas, but do *not* copy them. These should be very specific examples. Here is a sample:

I do this by   *example*

- Using real materials as often as possible to support the children's learning. Last week, they were wondering what kinds of fruit had the most seeds, so we all explored this question the next day by looking inside every type of fruit we could find at the market.

When your three examples are written, you are ready to look at Functional Area 6 on page 54 in your book. Leave a few spaces and type this:

Functional Area 6: Communication

Look on page 54 at the statement in the green box. You are going to rewrite it in *your own* words. Read the Developmental Context on page 54 for ideas. I may write something like this:

I encourage children to develop verbal and nonverbal skills by   *example*
offering many opportunities for them to express themselves,
to listen, and to interact with adults and each other.

You write it in *your own* words. Then type, "I do this by."
Now, write three specific examples of how *you* satisfy this goal in *your* program. You may look at the samples given in the book for ideas, but do *not* copy them. Here is a sample of a specific example:

I do this by   *example*

- Always sitting at the table with the children at mealtimes. I initiate and encourage conversations by asking open-ended questions. Sometimes we tell jokes or funny stories. Everyone enjoys this time together.

Now write three of your own. When your three examples are written, you are ready to look at Functional Area 7 on page 58 in your book. Leave a few spaces and type this:

Functional Area 7: Creative

Look at the statement in the green box. You are going to rewrite it in *your own* words. Read the Developmental Context on page 58 for ideas. I may write something like this:

example

In my classroom, children have many opportunities to express themselves creatively through the materials, activities, and props I provide.

You try writing it in *your own* words. Then type, "I do this by."

You will now write three specific examples of how *you* satisfy this goal in *your* program. You may look at the samples given in the book for ideas, but do *not* copy them. Here is a sample of a specific example:

example

I do this by

- Having several prop boxes, each with a different theme, such as Restaurant and Pet Shop. I bring out one of these boxes each Monday for the children to use to extend their dramatic and creative play.

After writing three examples, you will be finished with Competency Goal II. Check your word count to be sure it is near, but not more than, 500 words.

You are now ready to go on to Competency Goal III. Find it in on page 61 in your book. Start a new page. Begin Competency Goal III by copying what you see written, with the first line in bold type and the line below it in italics:

Competency Goal III
*To support social and emotional development
and to provide positive guidance*

Functional Area 8: Self

Look at the statement in the green box. You are going to rewrite it in *your own* words. Read the Developmental Context on page 61 for ideas. I may write something like this:

example

I provide opportunities for children to feel successful, to feel proud of themselves, and to do things independently. In my program, children feel safe, secure, and loved.

You try writing it in *your* own words. Then type, "I do this by."

Now write three specific examples of how *you* satisfy this goal in *your* program. You may look at the samples given in the book for ideas, but do *not* copy them. Here is a sample of a specific example:

example

Many times during the day, I give each child warm hugs "just because." Now they are not only spontaneously hugging me, but each other as well!

When your three examples are written, you are ready to look at Functional Area 9 on page 64 in your book. Leave a few spaces and type the following:

Functional Area 9: Social

Look at the statement in the green box. You are going to rewrite it in your own words. Read the Developmental Context on page 64 for ideas. I may write something like this:

> The children in my program are given opportunities to learn cooperation and social interaction. I encourage them to communicate and to get along with each other. *example*

You try writing it in *your own* words. Then type "I do this by."

Now write three specific examples of how *you* satisfy this goal in *your* program. You may look at the samples given in the book for ideas, but do *not* copy them. Here is a sample of a specific example:

> I do this by *example*
> - Emphasizing having fun and having everyone participate, rather than winning, when we play games, like soccer, outside.

When your three examples are written, you are ready to look at Functional Area 10 on page 66 in your book. Leave a few spaces and type this:

Functional Area 10: Guidance

Look at the statement in the green box. You are going to rewrite it in your own words. Read the Developmental Context on page 66 for ideas. I may write something like this:

> I help children learn to be self-disciplined through support, consistency, and positive role-modeling. *example*

You try writing it in *your own* words. Then type "I do this by."

Write three specific examples of how *you* satisfy this goal in *your* program. You may look at the samples given in the book for ideas, but do *not* copy them. Here is a sample of a specific example:

> I do this by *example*
> - Helping the children come up with a list of five simple rules, stated in positive terms, which we post on the wall:

1. Be kind to everyone.

2. Tell others how you feel.

3. Be a good listener.

4. Use walking feet.

5. Share with your friends.

All of our rules can be "read" by the children because they include pictures along with the words.

After writing three examples, you are finished with Competency Goal III. Check your word count to be sure it is up to, but not more than, 500 words.

You are ready to go on to Competency Goal IV. Find it in your book on page 69. Start a new page. Begin Competency Goal IV by copying what you see written, with the first line in bold type and the line below it in italics:

Competency Goal IV
To establish positive and productive relationships with families

Functional Area 11: Families

Look at the statement in the green box. You are going to rewrite it in *your own* words. Read the Developmental Context on page 69 for ideas. I may write something like this:

example

> I encourage the children's families to get involved in our activities whenever possible. I encourage and support a close relationship between home and school.

You try writing it in *your own* words. Then type "I do this by."
Now write specific examples of how *you* satisfy this goal in *your* program. You may look at the samples given in your book for ideas, but do *not* copy them. Here is a sample of a specific example:

example

I do this by

• Writing a newsletter every month for the families. In it, I cover what the children have been doing and learning. I try to refer to specific children by name, often quoting something they've said. I also preview upcoming activities and tell adult family members how they can get involved. My newsletter also includes a parenting tip or a fun activity that family members can do with their children at home.

You will notice that this sample is rather wordy. Since Competency Goal IV has only one Functional Area, your examples can go into greater detail. You will also need to include at least six or seven examples, instead of three, to bring the word count near 500 words. After writing your own examples, you are finished with Competency Goal IV. You are now ready to go on to Competency Goal V. Find it in your book on page 73. Start a new page. You will begin Competency Goal V by copying what you see written, with the first line in bold type and the line below it in italics:

Competency Goal V
To ensure a well-run, purposeful program
responsive to participant needs

Functional Area 12: Program Management

Look at the statement in the green box. You are going to rewrite it in *your own* words. Read the Developmental Context on page 73 for ideas. I may write something like this:

> I maintain a well-run program by being organized and observant, keeping accurate records, and developing long- and short-term plans.

example

You try writing it in *your own* words. Then type "I do this by."
Write specific examples of how *you* satisfy this goal in *your* program. You may look at the samples given in your book for ideas, but do *not* copy them. Here is a sample of a specific example:

> I do this by
>
> • Keeping a small spiral notebook in my pocket. In it, I record anecdotal notes on the children as they play, try new things, master skills, and interact with each other. I share these notes with the parents or guardians during conferences and use them for planning developmentally appropriate activities for the class.

example

Notice that this example is rather long. You will also notice that Competency Goal V consists of only this one Functional Area: Program Management. As a result, your examples can go into greater detail. You may need to include at least six or seven examples to bring the word count near 500 words. After writing your examples, you will be finished with Competency Goal V. Make sure the word count for this Competency Goal is near 500 words. You are now ready to go on to Competency Goal VI. Find it on page 76 in your book. Start a new page. Begin Competency Goal

VI by copying what you see written, with the first line in bold type and the line below it in italics:

Competency Goal VI
To maintain a commitment to professionalism

Functional Area 13: Professionalism

Look at the statement in the green box. You are going to rewrite it in *your own* words. Read the Developmental Context on page 76 for ideas. I may write something like this:

example

> I consider myself a professional and, as such, constantly seek additional education in child development and developmentally appropriate practice. I often attend workshops offered in my community as well as attend early childhood conferences. I aim to do the best I possibly can for the children and families in my program.

You try writing it in *your own* words. Then type "I do this by."

Now write about six or seven specific examples of how *you* satisfy this goal in *your* program. You may look at the samples given in your book for ideas, but do *not* copy them. Here is a sample of two specific examples:

example

> I do this by
>
> • Being a member of NAEYC and my local chapter. I work on the membership committee and encourage others to join and support young children through this organization.
>
> • Keeping all information about the children in my class and about their families confidential. I do not discuss personal information that parents or guardians may share with me, nor do I compare one child with another in front of parents or anyone else. I want the parents and guardians in my program to feel they can come to me with questions or concerns without worrying about the information being shared with others. By so doing, I can build strong connections between home and school, for the benefit of the children.

When you finish writing your six or seven specific examples for this Functional Area, you are finished with Competency Goal VI. Check your word count to be sure it is near 500 words.

You have now completed all six Competency Goal Statements and will put them into your Professional Resource File, behind the divider whose tab you labeled "Competency Goal Statements." You might want to put these sheets into page protectors, but before you do, make photocopies of them to give to the Council representative during your verification visit. Place these copies into the file folder or pocket folder where you have already placed a copy of your autobiography.

Congratulations! Your Professional Resource File is complete.

Preparing for the Assessment Observation by the CDA Advisor

The next step in your CDA process is to prepare for the assessment observation by your CDA advisor. With any luck, you have been able to locate an advisor of your own choosing, or you have contacted the Council for a listing of registered CDA advisors in your area.

The CDA advisor is the only person who will observe you working with young children in your program. The Council representative, on the other hand, will meet with you only to conduct the verification visit. She will *not* be observing.

Being prepared for your advisor's visit(s) is important. As soon as you receive your CDA application packet, it is a good idea to make a photocopy of the CDA Assessment Observation Instrument booklet. It is the stapled booklet with a yellow cover. Use it to do a self-study on your work with the children in your classroom, as well as on the classroom environment, before your advisor comes to do an observation.

Looking at your copied CDA Assessment Observation Instrument booklet, you will notice that each item is to be rated 3, 2, or 1. A rating of 3 means you can be observed complying with this item *most* of the time. A rating of 2 means you can be observed complying with this item *sometimes*. A rating of 1 means you can be observed *rarely* complying with this item.

As you go through your photocopied booklet and rate yourself, note any items rated below a 3 and write some notes in the margin to yourself about what is not up to par and how you plan to remedy the situation. Do not underestimate the importance of doing this self-study. It is important that you become familiar with the things your advisor will be looking for and on which you will be rated. You should come to work the day of your advisor's visit having prepared your classroom and yourself for a successful observation.

You need to be observed while working as *lead teacher* in a state-approved child development center with a group of at least eight children, all of whom are ages three through five. Even though you may not hold a lead teacher position at your workplace, you will need to be observed functioning in this capacity during your advisor's visits. After all, she wants to see *your* expertise and skill as a teacher, not someone else's. You will want to speak to your center director about this prior to your observations, so the person who is usually the lead teacher can temporarily give you that role. During the observations, your advisor will also assess your classroom environment based on national CDA standards. Ideally, the advisor visits at least once prior to conducting the official assessment observation. This will be an informal visit. She will look around, watch you in action with the children, and take notes. Afterward, she will share her observations, indicate problem areas, and suggest ways of improving.

The final observation will be a formal one and your advisor will not be able to offer any feedback to you about it. Your advisor will record her assessments, notes, and ratings in the yellow CDA Assessment Observation Instrument booklet. The items to be rated are arranged according to the Competency Goal Standards and Functional Areas.

It will not be possible for the advisor to observe *all* of the items in the Assessment Observation Instrument. Perhaps she will not be at your center during snacktime so she won't see the procedures you follow. In such a case, she will ask you about these items that were not observed and record your answers and comments. The formal observation may take as long as three hours.

After completing the observation and filling in the Assessment Observation Instrument booklet, your advisor will return the booklet to you, sealed in an envelope. It must *remain sealed* to be given to the Council representative when she visits you. If the seal on this Assessment Observation Instrument booklet is broken, the Council will not accept it. The assessment observation will have to be repeated, a new Assessment Observation Instrument booklet completed, and the verification visit rescheduled for a future date. All of this will cause an unnecessary delay in the award of your credential, perhaps by several months, so remember to simply keep the Assessment Observation Instrument booklet sealed in the envelope!

As you worked to complete your six Competency Goal Statements, you read over the listing of examples under each Functional Area in the green CDA book. These examples represent the criteria that define a successful CDA candidate. You also completed a self-study based on the items in the CDA Assessment Observation Instrument, as previously suggested. In addition to these valuable steps in preparing for your assessment observation, you will benefit from reading the program tips based on the CDA Competency Standards.

Program Tips

The areas in your room should be safe and free from hazards. Good health should be promoted.

- Sharp corners should be covered.

- Flimsy shelving should be removed.

- Electrical cords should be wound up and out of reach.

- Miniblind cords should be secured to the tops of windows.

- Small items that could be ingested should not be left out on tables or on the floor.

- Cleaners and chemicals should be secured and locked out of the reach of children.

- Area rugs should be secured to the floor to prevent tripping.

- Caregivers need to wash their hands before handling food, after assisting children in the restroom, and after wiping noses.

- Close supervision should be maintained at all times. Teachers should always position themselves so they have full view of the room and should never turn their backs on the children.

- The room should be generally clean and tidy.

- Restrooms should be sanitized daily. Liquid soap and disposable towels should be available for the children's use.

- Covered, plastic-lined trash cans should be available.

- Children should have separate storage for their own belongings.

- A simple escape route should be posted near the door.

- A chart of CPR and first-aid procedures should be posted.

- There should be a first-aid kit readily available in your room. If it is in a cabinet, the outside of the cabinet should be labeled "First Aid" to indicate where it is located.

- At least one fully charged fire extinguisher should be available nearby, and you should be trained in its use.

- Functioning smoke detectors should be installed.

- Good nutrition should be the focus of snacks and meals served. Processed foods and junk foods should not be served. Fruit juice, water, or milk should be the only beverage choices, no Kool-Aid or soda. Teachers should not have sodas or snack foods in the classrooms for themselves.

- When the children eat, the teachers should sit at the tables with them, modeling good table manners, encouraging them to try new foods, and engaging them in pleasant conversation.

Your room should be set up specifically for children.

- There should be a number of "centers" set up for the children.

- These centers may include a block area, a dramatic play or housekeeping area, a book corner, and a table or two for creative art or manipulatives. There should be ample periods of free-choice time offered daily when children are free to choose among these centers. Children should not be "herded" as a large group from one activity to another. For example, the entire group should not sit down at a table to do an art project. Art should be one of the options for two or three children during free-choice time.

- The surroundings should be bright, cheerful, and inviting to children. There should be lots of the children's art displayed at the children's eye level. Some items may be suspended from the ceiling. You may also have interesting posters and mobiles hung.

- There should be child-sized furniture for the children. This would include tables and chairs.

- There should be age-appropriate toys and materials for preschoolers. These should be stored on low shelves that the children can easily access and put away.

- There should be opportunities for dramatic play. You may have a child-sized kitchen set, doll beds, dolls, dress-up clothes, and other props.

- There should be a set of building blocks, preferably wood unit blocks, available to the children. The block area should include props, such as small people or animal figures, to encourage creative play.

- Some kind of book corner or shelves should include children's books that the children can look at whenever they like. These books may be from your own collection or borrowed weekly from the public library. Other literacy materials should also be made available as the children show readiness for them, such as child-sized pencils, various types of papers, markers, and washable stamp pads and stamps.

- The environment should be literacy rich. The items in the room should be labeled wherever possible (for example, a small sign on the door that reads "door").

- Children should be read to frequently every day.

- Cultural diversity should be promoted through multiethnic and multiracial dolls and pretend foods of other cultures in the housekeeping area, posters reflecting differences, and a collection of multicultural children's books.

- Both boys and girls should have opportunities and be encouraged to play in all areas of the room, free from gender bias.

- Adaptations and accommodations should be made for children with special needs.

There should be opportunities for both large- and small-motor development, as well as cognitive development.

- Age-appropriate manipulatives, puzzles, stacking and sorting toys, interlocking blocks, and playdough should be available.
- There should be a safe place for the children to engage in outdoor play with age-appropriate equipment, such as a climber, swings, a slide, riding toys, and balls.
- Alternate indoor, large-motor activities should be available in case of inclement weather.

Children should have opportunities for creative activities on a daily basis, using the creative arts materials.

- An easel with paint should be set up.
- Open-ended process art activities, such as collage, free-form cutting and pasting, or fingerpainting, should be offered. No crafts or coloring book pages should be allowed.

Children should have the opportunity to learn through play with hands-on activities.

- Learning about colors, for example, should be done by manipulating real items of different colors, not by drill or flash cards.
- Learning shapes and numbers should be done through tactile experiences or games, not through flash cards or drills.
- There should be opportunities for many sensory activities, such as cooking, using playdough, handling different textures, and practicing visual discrimination.
- Absolutely no worksheets should be used.
- There should be a variety of age-appropriate toys, materials, and activities.
- Discovery, exploration, and problem solving should be encouraged.
- Children's varied learning styles should be respected and supported by individualizing the activities.

Children should have regular, short, age-appropriate group or circle activities as well as individual interactions that encourage socialization between teacher and children and among the children themselves.

- Games should be played.
- Movement activities with or without props or music should be provided.
- Stories should be read on a regular basis.

- Both caregivers and children should have opportunities to engage in storytelling.
- Flannelboard stories should be used to provide variety in the presentation of books.
- Fingerplays should be introduced.
- Music should be incorporated into the daily schedule.
- Group activities should not include any type of drills, flash cards, or memorization.
- No videos or television should be allowed (or only on rare occasions).

Children should have predictable routines, although daily activities may be flexible to suit the children's needs and interests.

- Greet each child and adult individually upon arrival.
- Use songs and games to ease transitions from one activity to the next, giving children ample notice when a change is about to occur.
- Have an activity planned for children who finish/transition early so they do not have to wait for the rest of the group.
- Have daily lesson plans and the materials to carry them out on hand when needed.

Children should be given the opportunity to learn self-discipline in positive, supportive ways.

- Establish a few, simple rules with the children. Post them, using pictures to convey the ideas. The rules should be stated in *positive* terms, for example, "Use walking feet," rather than "Don't run."
- Use redirection whenever possible.
- Provide logical and natural consequences for misbehavior.
- Encourage children to use words to convey their feelings.
- Model cooperation, sharing, and proper behavior.
- Use a normal voice with the children. Never shout.
- Show ample affection to each child.
- Expect children to help maintain the environment by having them help pick up toys and clean up messes.
- Give children the opportunity to problem solve with each other. Don't be too eager to step in.
- Anticipate problems before they happen, if possible, by being observant.

Interact and play with the children indoors and outdoors.

- Teachers should not be working on lesson plans, cutting things out, chatting with coworkers, or being otherwise preoccupied while the children are present.

- Be a good listener. Ask lots of open-ended questions and be patient with children as they speak. Spend time talking with each child every day.

Develop a partnership with the families in your program.

- Communicate regularly, verbally and through newsletters and conferences.

- Invite family members to become involved in your program.

- Maintain a parent bulletin board with upcoming activities, parenting tips, child development information, and community resources available to them.

Maintain a well-run, organized program.

- Keep up-to-date health and emergency information files on each child in your care.

- Develop a brochure or leaflet for parents and guardians, outlining your center's policies, goals, services offered, and mission statement.

- Take anecdotal notes on each child.

- Keep a portfolio for each child that contains the anecdotal notes, samples of the child's art, and other evidence of skill development that can be shared with parents and guardians.

Maintain a commitment to professionalism.

- Join a national or local early childhood organization.

- Observe a strict policy of confidentiality with the families in your program.

- Continue to improve your skills by attending workshops or classes.

After your advisor has completed your assessment observation and all of your other documentation has been completed, you are ready to submit the Direct Assessment Application form. This indicates to the Council that you are ready for your verification visit.

Completing and Submitting the Direct Assessment Application Form

Does it matter when you send in your application?

No. Applications are now accepted on a rolling basis, which means there are no longer quarterly submission deadlines. Your verification visit will occur within ninety days of the Council receiving your application. Of course, this is assuming you completed the application correctly and included all of the necessary documentation. It is important to remember that your Parent Opinion Questionnaires and the Assessment Observation Instrument cannot be dated more than six months prior to the time the application form is sent in.

The Direct Assessment Application form came with your application packet, and it can be downloaded from the Council's website. The form is divided into eight sections. Section 1, Type of Assessment, is where you indicate your particular workplace setting. Check "Center-Based" and then "Preschool (3–5 years old)." You do not need to check "Monolingual" or "Bilingual" unless applicable. Under section 2, Type of Program, check the program type that best describes where you work.

Section 3 asks for your personal information. Section 4, Payment, asks you to indicate how the Direct Assessment fee is being paid, either directly by you or through an agency. If you are paying the fee yourself, you will need to send a check or money order with the application form.

In section 5, you are asked for a breakdown of your training hours into specific content areas, with at least ten clock hours per area:

1. Planning a safe, healthy learning environment
2. Steps to advance children's physical and intellectual development
3. Positive ways to support children's social and emotional development
4. Strategies to establish productive relationships with families
5. Strategies to manage an effective program operation
6. Maintaining a commitment to professionalism
7. Observing and recording children's behavior
8. Principles of child development and learning

Put the number of clock hours of training you have had in each of these eight subject areas in the boxes after the descriptions.

Often you can ask the agency or institution where you received this training to help you do this. Sometimes a course syllabus or outline of topics covered in a class or training session is also helpful. You can also look at the listing of subject areas with examples that is provided in appendix A on page 179.

You will need to acquire verification of the training sessions or the courses you have taken. This can be in the form of a certificate, an official letter on letterhead, or a transcript. The verification must also indicate the content area(s) of the training, the number of clock hours, and the name and address of the training institution or agency, and include an authorized signature. If your training occurred at several venues, you need this verification from each of them. Remember, the Council does not accept training hours obtained from conference workshops or consultants. Also in section 5, on the upper right, you are asked whether you received college credits for any of your training hours and, if so, how many. This item is easy to overlook, so be sure to complete it.

Section 6 asks you to verify certain things by making check marks next to each statement. One of the questions asks you to indicate that you have read the NAEYC Code of Ethical Conduct. This code provides a guide for conduct, practice, and ethical responsibility for early care and education providers. You received a copy of this document in the application packet. If you do not have a copy, you can download one from the NAEYC website (www.naeyc.org). Other questions in this section ask whether you have distributed and collected Parent Opinion Questionnaires, been observed by your advisor, and completed your Professional Resource File. You may not send in your application until you can check off these items as being completed.

If you have applied to the Council for any type of waiver, indicate this by checking the last box and attaching your Waiver Request form to the application. If you have applied for either a bilingual or monolingual assessment, you will fill in the last two items of section 6. Finally, sign and date the form, as indicated.

Your program director will complete and sign section 7 and your CDA advisor will complete section 8, indicating the date of the formal observation, noting the children's ages and program setting, and verifying that the CDA Assessment Observation Instrument was completed, put into a sealed envelope, and given to you.

When this form has been completed, retain the bottom copy for yourself. Then mail the application in with the designated payment, verification of training (including transcripts), description of the content of the training you had, and verification from your employer(s) of having at least 480 hours working with preschool-age children within the past five years. These are the *only* items that are to be sent with the application form. Do *not* send your Professional Resource File, Competency Goal Statements, autobiography, or Parent Opinion Questionnaires to the Council. You will need these items for your verification visit. It is smart to mail your application materials with a return receipt requested. This way, you will have confirmation that the Council received them.

You should receive a call from a Council representative within ninety days of sending in your application. If this much time has elapsed without any word, you may want to call the Council to verify that your application materials were received and that you are in the queue for the verification visit.

When the online application process becomes available, you can use this option instead of the traditional paper application. For additional information about the online application process, see pages 14–15.

Turn to chapter 6 on page 125 to read about the verification visit.

CDA Process: Center-Based Infant/Toddler

4

YOUR DECISION TO CARE FOR AND TEACH infants and toddlers is an important one. There is an increasing need for skilled and qualified caregivers for this age group. As many as 70 percent of children whose mothers work full-time are in some type of child care. Many of these families now depend on center-based care for their very young children.

Caring for infants and toddlers requires distinct training and skills because of the nature of these two age groups. In the past, working with infants and toddlers was viewed as "babysitting," but those who are responsible for the care and education of these children are early childhood professionals, no less than their counterparts working with preschool children. Daily routines constitute the curriculum in the infant or toddler program and are, of necessity, repetitive and constant. This work can, at times, be challenging and demanding on many levels, requiring a great deal of patience. Working with these very young children is also rewarding in many ways. These care providers are the ones who witness first steps, hear first words, and form loving attachments with our youngest children.

Infant/toddler care in a group setting is distinctly different from that of preschool children. It is not merely a small-scale form of preschool. Infants and toddlers experience accelerated changes in development and physical growth, more so than at any other time in their lives. These children are also defenseless against harm and distress and are totally dependent on their care providers for protection and consistent, loving care.

Part of these professionals' work is creating strong, reciprocal relationships with families. Optimal growth and development is achieved when close communication and coordination of effort occur between care providers and the children's families.

The CDA Competency Standards outline the skills that infant and toddler care providers need to meet the unique needs of these very young children. *The Child Development Associate Assessment System and Competency Standards for Infant/Toddler Caregivers in Center-Based Programs* (Council for Professional Recognition 2010) was recently revised to include the following:

- Restructured Competency Standards that reflect current research about supporting optimal infant and toddler development in early childhood centers

- Updated concepts and terminology

- Principles for supporting infants and toddlers who are dual-language learners

To gain or retain a position in a quality child development center, expect advancement, and seek proper compensation, you are pursuing a CDA Credential and becoming an early childhood professional. As such, you will need to demonstrate your competency in working with infants and toddlers. Having completed or nearly completed the 120 clock hours of training, you are ready to begin the remainder of the CDA process. Your Professional Resource File should now be set up and ready to fill with your Professional Resource Collection.

Assembling the Professional Resource Collection

You have already completed your autobiography, and it should be in the first section of your Professional Resource File. Next, type a label for the second divider page, whose tab you labeled "Competency Goal I." Type the label as follows:

> **COMPETENCY GOAL I**
> *To establish and maintain a safe,*
> *healthy learning environment*

Looking in your yellow CDA book, you will see this written in bold print on page 17. Notice that the first line is capitalized and the second line is italicized. You will do the same. Place the label in the center of the second divider page, whose tab you labeled

"Competency Goal I." Behind this second divider, insert four empty page protectors.

Now type a label to place on each of these page protectors. On the labels, type the numbered items listed under Competency Goal I. On the first label, for example, type the following, being sure to include the number:

> **1. Provide a summary of the legal requirements in your state regarding child abuse and neglect (including contact information for the appropriate agency) and also your program's policy regarding your responsibility to report child abuse and neglect.**

Now place the label on the upper right corner of the first empty page protector. You now know instantly what goes into that page protector. You can probably find this information in your state child care licensing regulations or from your state child abuse prevention agency. Remember to include the phone number to call for information or to report abuse. Also, find out what the policy for reporting child abuse is for your particular child care center. Type this up after the previous information under a heading, such as "My Program's Policies for Reporting Child Abuse." Print all of this and insert it into the first page protector. Make sure you position the information on the paper so that the label on the page protector isn't covering it.

Even when you have put all the resources into the page protectors, keep the labels on them, as it makes the CDA representative's job much easier. She can see, without a doubt, that all seventeen items are there and that your file is complete.

The second page protector in this section will have a label typed as follows:

> **2. Include the current certificate of completion of a certified pediatric first-aid training course (that includes treatment for blocked airway and providing rescue breathing for infants and young children). Certification must have been within the past three years.**

Now, place this label on the top right corner of the second page protector. You will make a copy of your first-aid certificate and insert it into this page protector.

The third page protector in this section will have a label typed as follows:

Make sure your training was for pediatric first aid, *not* adult first aid! Do not include a copy of your CPR certificate unless it is combined with your first-aid certificate. It was not requested, and the Council frowns on items being included in the Professional Resource File that were not asked for specifically.

You do *not* need to type the italicized words you see in parentheses (for example, *Cooperative Extension Service or Child Care Food Program*) on the label.

> **3. Use the Internet, the public library, or your program's professional library to obtain the name and contact information for an agency that supplies information on nutrition for children and/or nutrition education for families.**

Place this label on the third page protector at the top right. After you locate the requested information, type it, print it, and insert it into this page protector. The fourth page protector in this section will have a label typed as follows:

> **4. Provide a sample of your weekly plan that includes goals for children's learning and development, brief descriptions of planned learning experiences, and also accommodations for children with special needs (whether for children you currently serve or may serve in the future).**

You can use the weekly activity plan form you usually use in your program, perhaps enlarging it to accommodate the information that is required. Or you can use the sample Individual Weekly Activity Plan for Infants on page 186 or the sample Weekly Activity Plan for Toddlers on page 188. Infant care providers will focus on the developmental domains (physical, cognitive, creative, social/emotional) and the daily routines that constitute a typical day. Toddler care providers will be sure to address all of the typical learning areas, such as art, language/literacy, circle, fine/gross motor, dramatic play, math, and science.

You have now completed collecting resources for Competency Goal I and are ready to move on to Competency Goal II. Make a label for the third divider page, whose tab you have labeled "Competency Goal II." This label should read as follows:

> **COMPETENCY GOAL II**
> *To advance physical and intellectual competence*

Place the label in the center of the divider page. Then place four page protectors behind this divider. Only the first page protector needs to be labeled. Here's how the label on the first page protector should read:

> **5. Select four songs, fingerplays, word games, or poems that you can use to promote phonological awareness. Describe strategies to promote phonological awareness among children whose home language is other than English.**

Place this label on the top right corner of the first page protector. You can go to the library and look in the children's department to find what you need. Ask the librarian to show you the teachers' books section. You can also search the Internet for these items.

Phonological awareness means hearing the sounds of letters and words. For young children, choosing songs, word games, and poems with an abundance of rhyming words and/or alliteration will help them in this area. *Alliteration* means the repetition of the same or similar consonant sounds at the beginning of words, as in "The tiny tiger took a tumble." Children whose home language is not English will benefit from similar activities, but teachers can also include activities in their native languages.

You can either type the items yourself or print examples from the Internet. Your explanation of strategies for promoting phonological awareness with English-language learners (ELL) should be typed on a separate page. Put these pages in the four page protectors, back to back.

Now, make a label for the next resource item you will put in your file, typing it as follows:

> **6. Describe nine learning experiences that promote physical, cognitive, and creative development— three for young infants, three for mobile infants, and three for toddlers. Describe the goals, materials, and teaching strategies used.**

Add three more page protectors to this section, placing the label you just made in the upper right corner of the first one.

Describe the nine activities, three for each age group. For each activity, provide a title, a list of goals (what you want the children to do or learn), a list of materials needed, and the procedure for presenting the activity to children (step by step). Then explain how the activity promotes physical, cognitive, and creative development. It should look something like the following example for toddlers:

Activity for Toddlers

example

Title: Playdough Fun

Goals: Children will manipulate playdough using their hands and various utensils. They will use their language skills to talk about what they are experiencing and doing.

Materials: Playdough, trays, assorted wooden dowels, plastic spoons, child-sized table, and chairs

Procedure: Place playdough on trays with an assortment of wooden and plastic utensils. Give one tray to each child. Encourage the children to manipulate the playdough to create something of their own choosing. Encourage the children to talk about what they are doing and how the playdough looks and feels.

This activity supports physical development because the children use their hands to manipulate the playdough and utensils. They strengthen their small-motor skills while doing so.

This activity supports cognitive development because the children have opportunities to feel different textures, count pieces of playdough, learn different colors and shapes, and use language to talk about what they are doing.

This activity supports creative development because the children create something of their own choosing by manipulating the playdough any way they like.

Describe two more activities for toddlers, using this format. Next, using the same format, describe three activities appropriate for young infants. Finally, describe three activities appropriate for mobile infants. You will have a total of nine activities. Type the three activities for each age group on separate pages. Place the pages back to back in the page protectors.

You are now finished collecting resources for Competency Goal II and are ready to move on to Competency Goal III. Make a label for the fourth divider page, whose tab you labeled "Competency Goal III." This label should read as follows:

COMPETENCY GOAL III
*To support social and emotional development
and to provide positive guidance*

Place the label in the center of the divider page. Then place three page protectors behind this divider. The label for the first page protector should read like this:

> **7. Provide the titles, authors, publishers, copyright dates, and short summaries of ten age-appropriate children's books *that you use* to support development of children's self-concept and self-esteem and to help children deal with life's challenges.**

Place this label on the first page protector. Go to the library and ask the children's librarian to help you find these books. Be sure to choose books that have copyright dates less than ten years old. Books that help children deal with life challenges, such as death, moving to a new home, starting a new school, or welcoming a new baby, are known as *bibliotherapy* or *therapeutic* books. Do *not* cut and paste information from an Internet bookstore. These are to be books *you* have actually used with the children in *your* program and with which you are very familiar. Type the information requested on one or two pages and insert them back to back into the first page protector.

Next, type a label for the second page protector as follows:

> **8. Use the Internet, the public library, or your program's professional library to obtain at least two resources designed to assist teachers in constructively dealing with children with challenging behaviors (such as aggressive behavior like hitting or biting, or shyness).**

Place this label on the second page protector. Again, the librarian at your local library will be able to help you find the books and information you need. These will not be children's materials; they will be books or articles for *teachers*. Be sure to list at least two resources. Type the information and insert it into this page protector.

The third page protector should be labeled as follows:

> **9. Provide the name and telephone number of an agency in the community where you work for making referrals to family counseling.**

Be sure the agency you select is located in the community where you work and not merely a website or an agency somewhere in your state. Type the information and insert it into this page protector. You are now finished collecting resources for

Competency Goal III and are ready to move on to Competency Goal IV.

In the center of the fifth divider, whose tab you labeled "Competency Goal IV," place a label that reads as follows:

> **COMPETENCY GOAL IV**
> *To establish positive and productive relationships with families*

Behind this divider page, put two page protectors. Label the first page protector as follows:

> **10. Find out where to obtain resources, materials, and translation services for families whose home language is other than English. Provide the agency name and contact information.**

Locate the name of the local agency, along with its address and phone number. Find the name(s) of someone at the agency to contact for information. Type this information and insert it into this page protector.

The second page protector should be labeled as follows:

> **11. Document your program's policies that specify parents' responsibilities and what the program does for parents.**

You may find this information in your center's parent handbook or orientation materials. It may be helpful to format the information this way:

example

What My Program Does for Parents

- Provides their children with a warm, loving, and safe place to play and learn

- Provides their children with nutritious snacks and meals

- Provides their children with trained and qualified caregivers

- Provides parent or guardian meetings in which the adults can gain information about a variety of parenting topics and get acquainted with other families

What Parents Can Do for My Program

- Respect the center's illness policy

- Pick up their children on time

Remember, these are provided only as examples. You must use your own center's policies, specific to your program!

- Provide a complete change of clothing at the center in case of accidents
- Visit the classroom and participate with their child or children whenever possible

You are now finished collecting resources for Competency Goal IV and are ready to move on to Competency Goal V.

In the center of the sixth divider, whose tab you labeled "Competency Goal V," place this label:

> **COMPETENCY GOAL V**
> *To ensure a well-run, purposeful program*
> *responsive to participant needs*

Behind this divider, place three page protectors. Type a label that reads as follows to place on the first one.

> **12. Provide three samples of record-keeping forms used in early childhood programs. Include an accident report, an emergency form, and a third form of your choice.**

Be sure to include the two types of forms that are specifically requested: the accident report and the emergency form. The third form could be a registration form, an attendance sign-in sheet, a field-trip permission form, or a daily report form. Put each requested form in a separate page protector. You have now completed collecting resources for Competency Goal V and are ready to move on to Competency Goal VI.

In the center of the seventh divider, which you tabbed "Competency Goal VI," place a label that reads like this:

> **COMPETENCY GOAL VI**
> *To maintain a commitment to professionalism*

Behind this divider, place several page protectors. Type a label that reads as follows to place on the first one.

> **13. Use the Internet, the public library, or your program's professional library to obtain the name, address, and phone number of your state's agency that regulates child care centers and homes. Describe two important requirements related to your job responsibilities.**

Type only the name, address, and phone number of your state's child care regulating agency and place this page in the first page protector. Then go to the website listed below to look up the child care regulations for your particular state:

National Resource Center of Health and Safety in Child Care
http://nrckids.org/STATES/states.htm

Print out the section(s) that describes the qualification requirements for personnel (teachers, directors, and assistants). You will find this information in the regulations under "Staffing," "Personnel Policies," or something similar. Print only these particular sections for your file. In these sections, locate a listing of important requirements that are related to your own particular job responsibilities as a teacher, an assistant teacher, or a director and highlight them with a yellow highlighting marker. Now put these regulations in page protectors.

Choose two of the highlighted requirements and type them on a separate page with this title: "Requirements Related to My Job Responsibilities." Put this in the first labeled page protector, in front of the regulations.

Type a label for the next page protector that reads as follows:

> **14. Review the websites of two or three national early childhood associations (one with a local affiliate) to obtain information about membership, their resources, and how to order. Download at least two resources from the Internet that will enhance your work.**

These associations could include the National Association for the Education of Young Children (NAEYC, www.naeyc.org) or the National Association of Child Care Professionals (NACCP, www.naccp.org). Type the requested information about the two or three associations, and place it in the page protector. Be sure to include information about becoming a member, the types of resources that are available for download or purchase from each website, and how a person can order them.

Then find two articles on one of the websites that relate to your work with infants and toddlers. On the NAEYC website (www.naeyc.org), you can access back issues of *Young Children*, which has many articles from which to choose. Print two articles and put them back to back into page protectors.

The next page protector will be labeled as follows:

15. Obtain four pamphlets or articles designed to help parents understand how young children develop and learn. Articles must help parents understand how babies and toddlers (birth to age 3) develop and learn. At least one article must relate to brain development.

Put each pamphlet or article in its own page protector. Only the first page protector needs to be labeled. You can find some pamphlets like this at a pediatrician's office, your local hospital, the health department, or perhaps the public library. Articles may also be downloaded from the Internet. Be sure the pamphlets or articles you choose are written primarily for parents and address topics about how children grow and learn during the infant and toddler years. This could include information about stages of development and what parents can expect their child to be doing at specific ages. It would *not* include information about immunizations, dental or physical health, or safety. Do not include information about preschoolers or school-age children. Remember that one of the pamphlets or articles has to be about brain development and that you have been asked to include four items. Do *not* include more or less than four!

The next page protector will be labeled as follows:

16. Locate an observation tool to use in recording information about children's behavior. One copy should be blank; the other copy should be filled out as a sample of your observation of an individual child.

Use a form you typically use in your work with infants or toddlers. If you do not have such a form, you can use the observation tool provided on page 183. It is for recording an anecdotal record. An anecdotal record is a type of observation tool. It is a short written record based on observation of a child's behavior.

You may put both copies (one blank and one filled out) back to back in the same page protector. *Do not include the child's name on the observation.*

The next page protector will be labeled as follows:

17. Obtain contact information for at least two agencies in the community that provide resources and services for children with disabilities.

Find information on two or three agencies, which might include those that provide physical therapy, occupational therapy, speech therapy, or other developmental or learning services. In some communities, the local school district provides these services. Be sure these are local agencies that families enrolled in your program can access. Include the name of each agency, its address, phone number, and the name(s) of a person(s) who can be contacted for information. Type this information and insert it into this page protector.

If all of your page protectors are filled, the Professional Resource Collection section of your Professional Resource File is complete! Resist the temptation to add materials and information that were not specifically asked for in your yellow book. This will not impress the Council representative. On the contrary, it will indicate your inability to follow instructions and may interfere with the representative's ability to sort through the resources to determine whether your file is complete.

That being said, this Professional Resource File does belong to you. The Council representative will look it over and check it for accuracy but will not keep it. The Professional Resource Collection will be a valuable source of reference to you as a professional. After you receive your CDA Credential, you can continue to add resources to the original collection for your own personal use.

You are now ready to work on the third and final portion of the Professional Resource File: Competency Goal Statements. This is the last tabbed section of your file.

Writing the Competency Goal Statements

The national Competency Standards are used to evaluate a CDA candidate's skills in working with young children. Six Competency Goals within these standards state general goals for caregiver performance. Under each of the Competency Goals are one or more Functional Areas, for a total of thirteen. The thirteen Functional Areas define more specifically the skills and behaviors you must perform to meet each of the Competency Goals.

Your task will be to rewrite, in *your own* words and with *your own* individual understanding, each of the thirteen Functional Area statements. Next, you will provide several very specific examples from your own work with young children, which will demonstrate your competency in each of the Functional Areas.

Refer to pages 39–88 in your yellow CDA book. There you will see the Competency Goals written in yellow-tinted boxes, with the Functional Area statements in italics in gold boxes beneath them. Below that, each Functional Area is further defined by a Developmental Context or explanation for each of the three age groups: young infants, mobile infants, and toddlers. Finally, you will see a listing of examples of caregiver competence for each of the Functional Areas.

Look at pages 39–49 in your CDA book to find Competency Goal I. Notice that it has three Functional Areas: Safe, Healthy, and Learning Environment. Begin writing your first Competency Goal Statement by typing what you see written in the yellow box exactly as you see it, with the first line in bold print and the second line in italics:

Competency Goal I
To establish and maintain a safe,
healthy learning environment

Functional Area 1: Safe

Now, instead of writing what you see in the gold box in your book, you will need to rewrite it in *your own* words. Instead of writing "Candidate provides a safe environment to prevent and reduce injuries," you will personalize this statement in your own words. For some ideas on doing this, read the Developmental Context section under the Functional Area on page 39 in your yellow book. Here are two examples of what you might write:

> I make sure to provide a setting that promotes safety and minimizes the risk of injuries.   *example*

> Safety is a main priority in the environment I provide for the children in my care. I make every effort to prevent injuries and accidents.   *example*

You can see that I've included all the main ideas of the Council's version but in my own words. Now try writing *your own* version. Do not use the word *will* in the statement, because this is not something you *will* be doing, but rather something you are doing right now. So, if this were *my* Competency Goal Statement, it would look like this so far:

Competency Goal I   *example*
To establish and maintain a safe, healthy learning environment

Functional Area 1: Safe

Safety is a main concern in the environment that I provide for the children in my care. I make every effort to prevent injuries and accidents.

You will now give *specific* examples of things *you* do in *your* program to satisfy this goal. If you look in your yellow book, you will see a list of examples on pages 39–41. You may *not* copy these examples. They are meant to give you ideas. Also, they are much too general in nature. You should write examples that are specific to your own work with young children, in your program.

You will give two examples for each of the three age groups: young infants (birth through eight months), mobile infants (nine through seventeen months), and toddlers (eighteen through thirty-six months). For instance, one of the examples given in the book reads, "Anticipates and makes plans to prevent potentially dangerous situations." I may do things in *my* program to avoid dangerous situations, too, but what do I do specifically? After thinking about it, I write this heading:

Young Infants

Then I write a specific example of how I anticipate and plan to avoid dangerous situations with young infants:

example
> Keeping blankets, quilts, and stuffed animals out of the cribs to avoid the possibility of suffocation.

I will write one more example of something I do to keep young infants safe.

Now I will make another heading:

Mobile Infants

I will write two specific examples of how I keep mobile infants safe. And I make a third heading:

Toddlers

I will write two specific examples of how I keep toddlers safe. You can write them as a bulleted list or in a descriptive paragraph. If I chose to write the examples in a bulleted list, my completed statement for Functional Area 1: Safe would look like this:

example

Competency Goal I
To establish and maintain a safe, healthy learning environment

Functional Area 1: Safe

Safety is a main concern in the environment that I provide for the children in my care. I make every effort to prevent injuries and accidents.

Young Infants

I do this by

- Keeping blankets, quilts, and stuffed animals out of the cribs to avoid the possibility of suffocation.
- *(Another example).*

Mobile Infants

I do this by

- *(An example).*
- *(Another example).*

Toddlers

I do this by

- *(An example).*
- *(Another example).*

After writing *your own* examples, you are ready to begin your Competency Goal Statement for Functional Area 2. Leave a few spaces, and write this:

Functional Area 2: Healthy

On page 42 in your book, look at the statement written in the gold box outlined in black. It reads, "Candidate promotes good health and nutrition and provides an environment that contributes to the prevention of illness." Rewrite it in *your own* words, looking at the Developmental Context on page 42 for ideas. I might write something like this:

> I encourage proper nutrition and good health habits every day by modeling these behaviors and providing an environment that promotes them and where risk of illness is reduced.

example

You try writing it in *your own* words. After you do, type "I do this by."

You may now give some *specific* examples of things *you* do in *your* program to satisfy this goal. Do *not* copy the examples provided in your book, but do gain some ideas from them. One of these examples on page 43 in the book reads, "Makes sure play areas and materials are cleaned daily."

Here is a specific example I might write for mobile infants:

example

> At the end of each day, I wash all toys that were mouthed by the children in warm, soapy water. Those items that cannot be washed in the sink are sanitized with a safe, nontoxic spray and left to air-dry.

You will need to write two specific examples of your own under each of the three age groups: young infants, mobile infants, and toddlers. Use the format suggested previously.

When you finish your examples, you will be ready to begin your Competency Goal Statement for Functional Area 3. Leave a few spaces and write this:

Functional Area 3: Learning Environment

Look at the statement written in the gold box outlined in black on page 46 in your book. It reads, "Candidate uses space, relationships, materials, and routines as resources for constructing an interesting, secure, and enjoyable environment that encourages and fosters trust, play, exploration, interaction, and learning." Rewrite it in *your own* words, looking at the Developmental Context on page 46 for ideas. I might write something like this:

example

> The learning environment I provide encourages children to feel comfortable, to be curious, to explore, and to learn. This is done through interesting activities, materials, and opportunities for socialization.

You try writing it in *your own* words. After you do, type "I do this by."

Now you are ready to write *specific* examples of how *you* satisfy this goal in *your* program. Look at the samples given in the book on pages 46–49, using them for ideas. Again make three headings—one for young infants, one for mobile infants, and one for toddlers—providing two examples for each. Here is a sample of a specific example for toddlers:

example

> I put all the children's toys in open bins that are labeled with pictures. They are stored on low, open shelves so the children have easy access to them and quickly learn how to put the toys away themselves.

After writing your six examples for this Functional Area, you will be finished with Competency Goal I.

The writing you have done for this Competency Goal must add up to between 200 and 500 words. Count only the words in the Functional Area statements and the examples under each of them, not the words you copied from the yellow-tinted boxes. Please be sure to do a word count on your computer to be certain you are within this word-count range, as the Council is very particular about this. It is better to be closer to 500 words, because a thorough explanation of your competency is better than one that is too short and incomplete. That said, you should not go over 500 words, because the Council sees this as a failure to follow instructions and you will lose points. If your word count is well under 500 words, add additional examples under the Functional Areas. If you have more than 500 words, take out a couple of your examples.

Now you are ready to go on to Competency Goal II. Find it in your book on page 50. You will see that this Competency Goal has four Functional Areas: Physical, Cognitive, Communication, and Creative.

Begin Competency Goal II on a new page by copying what you see written in the yellow box, with the first line in bold print and the second line in italics:

Competency Goal II
To advance physical and intellectual competence

Functional Area 4: Physical

Now, rewrite what you see in the gold box outlined in black. It should be in your own words. Read the Developmental Context on page 50 for ideas. I might write something like this:

> In my program, children have daily opportunities, both indoors and outdoors, to participate in activities that enhance their physical development.

example

You try writing it in *your own* words. Then type "I do this by."

Now give two *specific* examples for each of the three age groups describing how *you* meet this goal in *your* program. Think of specific examples that may encourage small- or large-motor development. Look at the examples on pages 50–52 for ideas, but do *not* copy them. Here is a sample of a specific example:

Young Infants

example

I do this by

- Placing the infants on their tummies on a firm, carpeted surface so they can lift up and strengthen their upper bodies several times a day. I provide interesting, colorful toys with moving parts to encourage them to reach and move.

Write two examples of your own for young infants. Then write two examples for mobile infants and two for toddlers.

When you have finished writing your examples, you are ready to go on to Functional Area 5. Find Functional Area 5 on page 53 in your book. Leave a few spaces and type this heading:

Functional Area 5: Cognitive

Look at the statement in the gold box outlined in black. Write that statement in your own words. Read the Developmental Context on page 53 for ideas. I might write something like this:

example

> I feel it is important for children to exercise their curiosity and have opportunities to problem solve, so I provide an environment and developmentally appropriate activities that allow for discovery and exploration.

Now try writing it in *your own* words. Then type "I do this by."

Write examples of how *you* satisfy this goal in *your* program, two for each of the three age groups: young infants, mobile infants, and toddlers. Look at the samples given in your book for ideas, but do *not* copy them. Here is a sample of a specific example:

example

> **Mobile Infants**
>
> I do this by
>
> • Sometimes placing a colorful toy under the edge of a blanket while the children watch and then asking them where it went. I'll lift off the blanket and say, "Surprise!" They love this game and are learning the concept of object permanence.

Write two examples of your own for mobile infants. Then write two examples for young infants and two for toddlers. When you have finished writing your examples, you are ready to go on to Functional Area 6. Find Functional Area 6 on page 57 in your book. Leave a few spaces and type this:

Functional Area 6: Communication

Look at the statement in the gold box outlined in black. You are going to rewrite it in *your own* words. Read the Developmental Context on page 57 for ideas. I may write something like this:

example

> I encourage children to develop verbal and nonverbal skills by offering many opportunities for them to express themselves, to listen, and to interact with adults and each other.

You try writing it in *your own* words. Then type "I do this by."

Now, write examples of how *you* satisfy this goal in *your* program, two for each of the three age groups: young infants, mobile infants, and toddlers. You may look at the samples given in your book for ideas, but do *not* copy them. Here is a sample of a specific example:

Toddlers

example

I do this by

- Always sitting at the table with the children at mealtimes. I initiate and encourage conversation by asking open-ended questions. Sometimes we tell jokes or funny stories. Everyone enjoys this time together.

Write two examples of your own for toddlers. Then write two examples for young infants and two for mobile infants. When you have finished writing your examples, you are ready to go on to Functional Area 7. Find Functional Area 7 on page 61 in your book. Leave a few spaces and type this:

Functional Area 7: Creative

Look at the statement in the gold box outlined in black. You are going to rewrite it in *your own* words. Read the Developmental Context on page 61 for ideas. I may write something like this:

example

In my classroom, children have many opportunities to express their individual creativity through the materials, activities, and props I provide.

You try writing it in *your own* words. Then type "I do this by."

Now you will write examples of how *you* satisfy this goal in *your* program, two for each of the three age groups: young infants, mobile infants, and toddlers. You may look at the samples given in your book for ideas, but do *not* copy them. These should be very *specific* examples. Here is a sample of a specific example:

Mobile Infants

example

I do this by

- Playing recordings of music with different tempos and rhythms. I hold the children's hands and we move and sway to the music. They can also choose instruments to play while we listen to the music.

Write two examples of your own for mobile infants. Then write two examples for young infants and two for toddlers. After writing your examples, you will be finished with Competency Goal II. Check your word count to be sure it is near 500 words but not more than that!

You are now ready to begin Competency Goal III. You can find it on page 64 in your yellow book. Start a new page. Begin Competency Goal III by copying what you see written in the yellow box, with the first line in bold type and the line below it in italics:

Competency Goal III
*To support social and emotional development
and to provide positive guidance*

Functional Area 8: Self

Look at the statement in the gold box outlined in black. You are going to rewrite it in *your own* words. Read the Developmental Context on page 64 for ideas. I may write something like this:

example
> I provide opportunities for children to feel successful, to feel proud of who they are, and to do things independently. In my program, children feel safe, secure, and loved.

You try writing it in *your own* words. Then type "I do this by."

Now write examples of how *you* satisfy this goal in *your* program, two for each of the three age groups: young infants, mobile infants, and toddlers. You may look at the samples given in your book for ideas, but do *not* copy them. Here is a sample of a specific example:

example
> **Toddlers**
>
> I do this by
>
> • Giving each child warm hugs "just because" many times during the day. Now they are not only spontaneously hugging me, but each other as well!

Write two examples of your own for toddlers. Then write two examples for young infants and two for mobile infants.

When you have finished writing your examples, you are ready to go on to Functional Area 9. Find Functional Area 9 on page 68 in your book. Leave a few spaces and type the following:

Functional Area 9: Social

Look at the statement in the gold box outlined in black. You are going to rewrite it in *your own* words. Read the Developmental Context on page 68 for ideas. I may write something like this:

example
> The children in my program are given opportunities to learn cooperation, respect, and social interaction. They are encouraged to communicate and to get along with each other.

You try writing it in *your own* words. Then type "I do this by."

Now write *specific* examples of how *you* satisfy this goal in *your* program, two for each of the three age groups: young infants, mobile infants, and toddlers. Look at the samples given in your book for ideas, but do *not* copy them. Here is a sample of a specific example:

Mobile Infants

example

I do this by

- Providing duplicates of our favorite toys, such as the fire truck and the pop-up boxes, so one child doesn't have to wait for another child to finish playing and the children don't get into conflicts over one toy.

Write two examples of your own for mobile infants. Then write two examples for young infants and two for toddlers.

When you have finished writing your examples, you are ready to go on to Functional Area 10. Find Functional Area 10 on page 71 in your book. Leave a few spaces and type this:

Functional Area 10: Guidance

Look at the statement in the gold box outlined in black. You are going to rewrite it in *your own* words. Read the Developmental Context on page 71 for ideas. I may write something like this:

I help children learn to be self-disciplined through encouragement and consistency and by being a positive role model. I provide patient and loving support for children struggling with difficult behaviors.

You try writing it in *your own* words. Then type "I do this by."

Now write *specific* examples of how *you* satisfy this goal in *your* program, two for each of the three age groups: young infants, mobile infants, and toddlers. Look at the samples given in your book for ideas, but do *not* copy them. Here is a sample of a specific example:

Young Infants

example

I do this by

- Responding immediately to an infant when he or she wakes and begins to fuss after a nap. This helps the child learn to trust me.

Write two examples of your own for young infants. Then write two examples for mobile infants and two for toddlers. After writing your examples, you will be finished with Competency Goal III.

Check your word count to be sure it is up to, but not more than, 500 words.

You are ready to go on to Competency Goal IV. Find it in your book on page 75. Start a new page. Begin Competency Goal IV by copying what you see written in the yellow box, with the first line in bold type and the line below it in italics:

Competency Goal IV

To establish positive and productive relationships with families

Functional Area 11: Families

Look at the statement in the gold box outlined in black. You are going to rewrite it in *your own* words. Read the Developmental Context on page 75 for ideas. I may write something like this:

example

> I encourage the children's families to get involved in our activities whenever possible. I encourage and support a close relationship between home and school.

You try writing it in *your own* words. Then type "I do this by."

Now write *specific* examples of how *you* satisfy this goal in *your* program, two for each of the three age groups: young infants, mobile infants, and toddlers. Look at the samples given in your book for ideas, but do *not* copy them. Here is a sample of a specific example:

example

Young Infants

I do this by

- Sending home a personalized sheet about each infant describing feeding times and amounts eaten, diapering information, how we played, what the child enjoyed, and a suggestion or two for the families so they can stimulate development at home.

Write two examples of your own for young infants. Then write two examples for mobile infants and two for toddlers.

When you have finished writing your examples, you are ready to go on to Competency Goal V. Find Competency Goal V on page 79 in your book. Start a new page. You will begin Competency Goal V by copying what you see written in the yellow box, with the first line in bold type and the line below it in italics:

Competency Goal V

To ensure a well-run, purposeful program responsive to participant needs

Functional Area 12: Program Management

Look at the statement in the gold box outlined in black. You are going to rewrite it in *your own* words. Read the Developmental Context on page 79 for ideas. I may write something like this:

> I maintain a well-run program by being organized and observant, keeping accurate records, and developing long- and short-term plans.

example

You try writing it in *your own* words. Then type "I do this by."
Write *specific* examples of how *you* satisfy this goal in *your* program. You may look at the samples given in your book for ideas, but do *not* copy them. Here is a sample of a specific, detailed example:

> I do this by

example

> • Keeping a small spiral notebook in my pocket. In it, I record anecdotal notes on the children as they play, try new things, master skills, and interact with each other. I share these notes with the parents or guardians during conferences and use them for planning developmentally appropriate activities for the children.

You will notice that this sample is rather wordy. Since Competency Goal V has only one Functional Area, your examples can go into greater detail. You will also need to include at least six or seven examples, instead of three, to bring the word count near 500 words. After writing your own six or seven examples, you will be finished with Competency Goal V. Make sure the word count for this Competency Goal is near 500 words. You are now ready to go on to Competency Goal VI. Find it on page 82 in your book. Start a new page. Begin Competency Goal VI by copying what you see written in the yellow box, with the first line in bold type and the line below it in italics:

For Functional Area 12: Program Management and Functional Area 13: Professional Development, you will not need to provide separate examples for each of the three age groups (young infants, mobile infants, and toddlers), as you did for Functional Areas 1 through 11. These final two Functional Areas refer to things you do to maintain a quality program and to increase your own professionalism, which affect all of the age groups as a whole.

Competency Goal VI
To maintain a commitment to professionalism

Functional Area 13: Professionalism

Look at the statement in the gold box outlined in black. You are going to rewrite it in *your own* words. Read the Developmental Context on page 82 for ideas. I may write something like this:

> I consider myself a professional and, as such, constantly seek additional education in child development and developmentally appropriate practice. I often attend workshops offered in my community as well as attend

example

early childhood conferences. I aim to do the best I possibly can for the children and families in my program.

You try writing it in *your own* words. Then type "I do this by."

Now write six or seven *specific* examples of how *you* satisfy this goal in *your* program. You may look at the samples given in your book for ideas, but do *not* copy them. Here is a sample of two specific examples:

example

I do this by

- Being a member of NAEYC and my local chapter. I work on the membership committee and encourage others to join and support young children through this organization.

- Keeping all information about the children in my class and about their families confidential. I do not discuss personal information that parents or guardians may share with me, nor do I compare one child with another in front of parents or anyone else. I want the parents and guardians in my program to feel they can come to me with questions or concerns without worrying about the information being shared with others. By so doing, I can build strong connections between home and school, for the benefit of the children.

When you finish writing your six or seven specific examples for this Functional Area, you will be finished with Competency Goal VI. Check your word count to be sure it is near 500 words.

You have now completed all six Competency Goal Statements and will put them into your Professional Resource File behind the divider whose tab is labeled "Competency Goal Statements." You might want to put these sheets into page protectors, but before you do, make photocopies of them to give to the Council representative during your verification visit. Place these copies into the file folder or pocket folder where you have already placed a copy of your autobiography.

Congratulations! Your Professional Resource File is complete.

Preparing for the Assessment Observation by the CDA Advisor

The next step in your CDA process is to prepare for the assessment observation by your CDA advisor. With any luck, you have been able to locate an advisor of your own choosing, or you have contacted the Council for a listing of registered CDA advisors in your area.

The CDA advisor is the only person who will visit and observe you working with young children in your program. The Council representative, on the other hand, will meet with you only to conduct the verification visit. She will *not* be observing.

Being prepared for your advisor's visit(s) is important. As soon as you receive your CDA application packet, it is a good idea to make a copy of the CDA Assessment Observation Instrument booklet. It is the stapled booklet with a yellow cover. Use it to do a self-study on your work with the children in your classroom, as well as on the classroom environment, before your advisor comes to do an observation.

Looking at the CDA Assessment Observation Instrument booklet, you will notice that each item is to be rated 3, 2, or 1. A rating of 3 means you can be observed complying with this item *most* of the time. A rating of 2 means you can be observed complying with this item *sometimes*. A rating of 1 means you can be observed *rarely* complying with this item.

As you go through your photocopied booklet and rate yourself, if you note any items rated below a 3, write some notes in the margin to yourself about what is not up to par and how you plan to remedy the situation. Do not underestimate the importance of doing this self-study. It is important that you become familiar with the things your advisor will be looking for and on which you will be rated. You should come to work the day of your advisor's visit having prepared your classroom and yourself for a successful observation.

You need to be observed while working as *lead teacher* in a state-approved child development center with a group of at least three children, all of whom are between the ages of birth and three years. Even though you may not hold a lead teacher position at your workplace, you will need to be observed functioning in this capacity during your advisor's visits. After all, she wants to see *your* expertise and skill as a teacher, not someone else's. You will want to speak to your center director about this prior to your observations, so the person who is usually the lead teacher can temporarily give you that role. During the observations, your advisor will also assess your classroom environment based on national CDA standards.

Because you are earning an infant/toddler CDA Credential, your advisor will need to observe you with all three age groups: young infants, mobile infants, and toddlers. Chances are that you typically work with only one of these age groups at your center. Whichever age group that is will be the group with which you will be observed working as a lead teacher. This will be the observation that the advisor records in the Assessment Observation Instrument booklet.

In your application packet, you will find a Supplemental Observation form. This is to be used by the advisor to record an observation of your work with the other two age groups, one at a time. For these supplemental observation, you do not have to be working as a lead teacher, but you will need to be fully involved with at least one child in each of the other two age groups for as long as two hours. Your advisor will observe you with a child from one age group and then with a child from the other age group. These should be children with whom you are familiar. You will participate in their daily routines, such as diapering, play, and mealtime. She can record both of these observations on the one Supplemental Observation form by dividing each of the sections. Or she can copy the form and use a separate one for each of the two age groups.

If, by chance, you typically work with two of the age groups in the same room, then your advisor will need to do only one supplemental observation. The Council requires that the same advisor complete all of your observations.

In some instances, a child care center may care for only toddlers and not infants. If this is the case in your situation, you may be observed with young infants and mobile infants at another location. This can be another center-based program or a family child care center. You should plan to visit the center before you are to be observed by your advisor. This visit will help you become familiar with the children and allow you to request permission from the director for your advisor to observe you there.

Ideally, the advisor visits you at least once prior to conducting the official assessment observation. This will be an informal visit. She will look around, watch you in action with the children, and take notes. Afterward, she will share her observations, indicate problem areas, and suggest ways of improving.

The final observations will be formal ones and your advisor will not be able to offer any feedback to you about them. Your advisor will record her assessments, notes, and ratings in the yellow CDA Assessment Observation Instrument booklet and on the Supplemental Observation forms. The items to be rated are arranged according to the Competency Goal Standards and Functional Areas.

It will not be possible for the advisor to observe *all* of the items on the Assessment Observation Instrument and Supplemental Observation forms. Perhaps she will not be at your center at snacktime, so she won't see the procedures you follow.

In such a case, she will ask you about these items that were not observed and record your answers and comments. The formal observation may take as long as three hours.

After completing the observations of your work with all three age groups, your advisor will return the Assessment Observation Instrument booklet with the Supplemental Observation forms attached to you. It will be sealed in an envelope. It must *remain sealed* to be given to the Council representative when she visits you. If the seal on this Assessment Observation Instrument booklet is broken, the Council will not accept it. The assessment observations will have to be repeated by an advisor, who will need to complete a new Assessment Observation Instrument booklet and Supplementary Observation forms. The verification visit will have to be rescheduled for a future date. All of this will cause an unnecessary delay in the award of your credential, perhaps by several months, so remember to simply keep the Assessment Observation Instrument booklet sealed in the envelope!

As you worked to complete your six Competency Goal Statements, you read over the listing of examples under each Functional Area in the yellow CDA book. These examples represent the criteria that define a successful CDA candidate. You also completed a self-study based on the items in the CDA Assessment Observation Instrument, as previously suggested. In addition to these valuable steps in preparing for your assessment observation, you will benefit from reading the program tips based on the CDA Competency Standards.

Program Tips

The areas in your room should be safe and free from hazards. Good health should be promoted.

- Sharp corners should be covered.

- Flimsy shelving should be removed.

- Electrical cords should be wound up and out of reach.

- Miniblind cords should be secured to the tops of windows.

- Small items that could be ingested should not be left out on tables or on the floor.

- Cleaners and chemicals should be secured and locked out of the reach of children.

- Area rugs should be secured to the floor to prevent tripping.

- Caregivers should wash their hands before handling food, after assisting children in the restroom, and after wiping noses.

- Toys should be continually washed and sanitized throughout the day as they are "mouthed" by the children.

- High chairs should be washed and sanitized after each use, including the seat, frame, and tray.

- Close supervision should be maintained at all times. Teachers should always position themselves so that they have full view of the room and should never turn their backs on the children.

- The room should be generally clean and tidy.

- Restrooms should be sanitized daily. Liquid soap and disposable towels should be available for the children's use, as well as low sinks, so toddlers can learn to wash their hands independently.

- Covered, plastic-lined trash cans should be available, one specifically for soiled diapers. Remove the soiled diapers often, so there is never an odor permeating the diapering area or room.

- Be familiar with and use safe sleeping positions with infants, either side or back placement.

- Keep blankets, quilts, and toys out of cribs.

- Children should be fully attended on a changing table. Make sure all supplies needed are within reach prior to beginning a diaper change.

- Make sure there are no cracks or tears on the surface of the changing table pad, even if a sheet of paper is used under the child when diapering. Do not use any type of tape in an attempt to repair it; just replace it.

- Label each child's box of moist diaper wipes and diaper rash cream with his or her name to avoid cross-contamination.

- Children should have separate storage for their own belongings. Never store belongings in a child's crib.

- A simple escape route should be posted near the door.

- A chart of CPR and first-aid procedures should be posted.

- There should be a first-aid kit readily available in your room. If it is in a cabinet, the outside of the cabinet should be labeled "First Aid" to indicate where it is located.

- At least one fully charged fire extinguisher should be available nearby, and you should be trained in its use.

- Functioning smoke detectors should be installed.

- Good nutrition should be the focus of snacks and meals served. Processed foods and junk foods should not be served. Fruit juice, water, or milk should be the only beverage choices. No Kool-Aid or soda. Teachers should not have sodas or snack foods in the classrooms for themselves.

- When the children eat, the teachers should sit at the tables with them, modeling good table manners, encouraging them to try new foods, and engaging them in pleasant conversation.

- Keep each child's formula labeled in the refrigerator. Half-used bottles or baby food jars should not be seen sitting around the room, but should be discarded promptly after feeding.

- Infants are held for feedings. They should not be in an infant seat or crib with a propped bottle at any time.

Your room should be set up specifically for children.

- There should be a number of "centers" set up for the children.

- These centers may include a block area, a dramatic play or housekeeping area, a book corner, and a table or two for creative art or manipulatives.

- There should be ample periods of free-choice time offered daily when children are free to choose among these centers. Children should not be "herded" as a large group, from one activity to another. For example, the entire group should not sit down at a table to do an art project. Art should be one of the options for two or three children, during free-choice time.

- The surroundings should be bright, cheerful, and inviting to children. There should be lots of the children's art displayed at the children's eye level. Some items may be suspended from the ceiling. You may also have interesting posters and mobiles hung.

- There should be child-sized furniture for the children. This would include tables and chairs.

- There should be age-appropriate toys and materials for young infants, mobile infants, or toddlers, depending on the age group in your care. These should be stored on low shelves so that the children can easily access toys and put them away.

- Provide duplicates of popular toys to discourage conflicts.

- There should be opportunities for dramatic play. You may have a child-sized kitchen set, doll beds, dolls, dress-up clothes, and other props.

- There should be a set of building blocks, preferably wood unit blocks, available to the children. The block area should include props, such as people or animal figures, to encourage creative play.

- Some kind of book corner or shelves should include cloth and board books that very young children can look at whenever they like. These books may be from your own collection or borrowed weekly from the public library. Other literacy materials should also be made available as the children show readiness for them, such as child-sized pencils, various types of papers, washable markers, and chubby crayons.

- The environment should be literacy rich. The items in the room should be labeled wherever possible (for example, a small sign on the door that reads "door").

- Children should be read to frequently every day.

- Include a variety of music in the environment, including singing.

- Spend time with individual children, on their level, at every opportunity, engaging them in play.

- Move nonmobile infants to different areas of the room throughout the day, changing their positions and perspectives.

- Provide safe, open floor space for exploration and movement.

- Provide items that encourage independence for toddlers, such as step stools at the sink and Velcro closures on paint smocks.

- Talk with individual children as you work through their daily routines, encouraging them to listen and respond. Use these times as opportunities for verbal interaction and bonding.

- Practice primary caregiving, whenever possible.

- Cultural diversity should be promoted through multiethnic and multiracial dolls and pretend foods of other cultures in the housekeeping area, posters reflecting differences, and a collection of multicultural children's books.

- Both boys and girls should have opportunities and be encouraged to play in all areas of the room, free from gender bias.

- Adaptations and accommodations should be made for children with special needs.

There should be opportunities for both large- and small-motor development, as well as cognitive development.

- Age-appropriate manipulatives, puzzles, stacking and sorting toys, interlocking blocks, and playdough should be available.

- There should be a safe place for the children to engage in outdoor play with age-appropriate equipment, such as a climber, swings, a slide, riding toys, and balls.

- Infants should be provided with time outdoors whenever weather permits.

- Alternate indoor, large-motor activities should be available in case of inclement weather.

- Infants should be given periods of "tummy time" every day on a floor surface under close supervision.

Children should have opportunities for creative activities on a daily basis, utilizing the creative arts materials.

- An easel with paint should be set up.

- Open-ended process art activities, such as collage, free-form cutting and pasting, or fingerpainting, should be offered. No crafts or coloring book pages should be allowed.

- Infants should be provided with objects to bat and kick, toys that respond to touch and movement.

Children should have the opportunity to learn through play with hands-on activities.

- Learning about colors, for example, should be done by manipulating real items of different colors, not by drill or flash cards.

- Learning shapes and numbers should be done through tactile experiences or games, not through flash cards or drills.

- There should be opportunities for many sensory activities, such as cooking, using playdough, handling different textures, and practicing visual discrimination.

- Absolutely no worksheets should be used.

- Discovery, exploration, and problem solving should be encouraged.

- Children's varied learning styles and abilities should be respected and supported, by individualizing the activities.

Children should have regular, short, age-appropriate group or circle activities as well as individual interactions that encourage socialization between teacher and children and among the children themselves.

- Games should be played.

- Movement activities with or without props or music should be provided.

- Stories should be read on a regular basis.

- Both caregivers and children should have opportunities to engage in storytelling.

- Flannelboard stories should be used to provide variety in the presentation of books.

- Fingerplays should be introduced.

- Music should be incorporated into the daily schedule.

- Group activities should not include any type of drills, flash cards, or memorization.

- No videos or television should be allowed.

- Cribs should be used only for sleeping. An infant should be out of the crib when awake, being held by the caregiver, placed in a swing for short periods, or positioned on a prepared area of the floor to play and exercise.

- Infant seats, bouncers, and mechanical swing devices should not be overused or used as a substitute for human contact.

Children should have predictable routines, although daily activities may be flexible to suit the children's needs and interests.

- Greet each child and adult individually upon arrival.

- Use songs and games to ease transitions from one activity to the next, giving children ample notice when a change is about to occur.

- Have an activity planned for children who finish/transition early, so they do not have to wait for the rest of the group.

- Create a weekly activity plan for toddlers based on their daily routines.

- Create a daily activity plan for each infant based on individual schedule and needs. Infants should not have their schedules altered, for example, being awakened from a nap to take a walk in the stroller.

Children should be given the opportunity to learn self-discipline in positive, supportive ways.

- Establish a few, simple rules with the children. Post them, using pictures to convey ideas. The rules should be stated in positive terms, for example, "Use walking feet," rather than "Don't run."

- Use redirection whenever possible with toddlers.

- Provide logical and natural consequences for misbehavior.

- Encourage children to use words to convey their feelings.

- Model cooperation, sharing, and proper behavior.

- Use a normal voice with the children. Never shout.

- Show ample affection to each child.

- Expect children to help maintain the environment by having them help pick up toys and clean up messes.

- Give children the opportunity to problem solve with each other. Don't be too eager to step in.

- Anticipate problems before they happen, if possible, by being observant.

Interact and play with the children indoors and outdoors.

- Teachers should not be working on lesson plans, cutting things out, chatting with co-workers, or acting otherwise preoccupied while the children are present.

- Upon waking, infants should be responded to promptly and taken from their cribs.

- Be a good listener. Ask lots of open-ended questions and be patient with children as they try to respond and speak. Spend time talking with each child every day.

Develop a partnership with the families in your program.

- Communicate regularly, verbally, and through newsletters and conferences.

- Invite family members to become involved in your program.

- Maintain a parent bulletin board with upcoming activities, parenting tips, child development information, and community resources available to them.

Maintain a well-run, organized program.

- Keep up-to-date health and emergency information files on each child in your care.

- Develop a brochure or leaflet for parents and guardians, outlining your center's policies, goals, services offered, and mission statement.

- Take anecdotal notes on each child.

- Keep a portfolio for each child that contains the anecdotal notes, samples of the child's art, and other evidence of skill development that can be shared with parents and guardians.

Maintain a commitment to professionalism.

- Join a national or local early childhood organization.

- Observe a strict policy of confidentiality with the families in your program.

- Continue to improve your skills by attending workshops or classes.

After your advisor has completed your assessment observation and all of your other documentation has been completed, you are ready to submit the Direct Assessment Application form. This indicates to the Council that you are ready for your verification visit.

Completing and Submitting the Direct Assessment Application Form

Does it matter when you send in your application?

No. Applications are now accepted on a rolling basis, which means there are no longer quarterly submission deadlines. Your verification visit will occur within ninety days of the Council receiving your application. Of course, this is assuming you completed the application correctly and included all of the necessary documentation. It is important to remember that your Parent Opinion Questionnaires and the Assessment Observation Instrument cannot be dated more than six months prior to the time the application form is sent in.

The Direct Assessment Application form came with your application packet, and it can be downloaded from the Council's website. The form is divided into eight sections. Section 1, Type of Assessment, is where you will indicate your particular workplace setting. You will check "Center Based" and then "Infant/Toddler (birth to 36 months old)." You will not need to check "Monolingual" or "Bilingual" unless applicable. Under section 2, Type of Program, check the program type that best describes where you work.

Section 3 asks for your personal information. Section 4, Payment, asks you to indicate how the Direct Assessment fee is being paid, either directly by you or through an agency. If you are paying the fee yourself, you will need to send a check or money order with the application form.

In section 5, you are asked for a breakdown of your training hours into specific content areas, with at least ten hours per area:

1. Planning a safe, healthy learning environment

2. Steps to advance children's physical and intellectual development

3. Positive ways to support children's social and emotional development

4. Strategies to establish productive relationships with families

5. Strategies to manage an effective program operation

6. Maintaining a commitment to professionalism

7. Observing and recording children's behavior

8. Principles of child development and learning

Put the number of clock hours of training you have had in each of these eight subject areas in the boxes after the descriptions. Often you can ask the institution or agency where you received this training to help you do this. Sometimes a course syllabus or outline of topics covered in a class or training session is also helpful. You can also look at the listing of subject areas with examples that is provided in appendix A on page 179.

You will need to acquire verification of the training sessions or the courses you have taken. This can be in the form of a certificate, official letter on letterhead, or a transcript. The verification must also indicate the content area(s) of the training, the number of clock hours, and the name and address of the training institution or agency, and include an authorized signature. If your training occurred at several venues, you will need this verification from each of them. Remember, the Council does not accept training hours obtained from consultants or conference workshops. Also in section 5, on the upper right, you are asked whether you received college credits for any of your training hours and, if so, how many. This item is easy to overlook, so be sure to complete it.

Section 6 asks you to verify certain things by making check marks next to each statement. One of the questions asks you to indicate that you have read the NAEYC Code of Ethical Conduct. This code provides a guide for conduct, practice, and ethical responsibility for early care and education providers. You received a copy of this document in the application packet. If you do not have a copy, you can download one from the NAEYC website (www .naeyc.org). Other questions in this section ask whether you have distributed and collected Parent Opinion Questionnaires, been observed by your advisor, and completed your Professional Resource File. You may not send in your application until you can check off these items as being completed.

If you have applied to the Council for any type of waiver, indicate this by checking the last box and attaching your Waiver Request form to the application. If you have applied for either a bilingual or monolingual assessment, you will fill in the last two items of section 6. Finally, sign and date the form, as indicated.

Your program director will complete and sign section 7 and your CDA advisor will complete section 8, indicating the date of the formal observation, noting the children's ages and program setting, and verifying that the CDA Assessment Observation Instrument was completed, put into a sealed envelope, and given to you.

When this form has been completed, keep the bottom copy for yourself. Then mail the application in with the designated payment, verification of training (including transcripts), description of the content of the training you had, and verification from your employer(s) of having at least 480 hours working with infants and/or toddlers within the past five years. These are the *only* items that are to be sent with the application form. Do *not* send your Professional Resource File, Competency Goal Statements, autobiography, or Parent Opinion Questionnaires to the Council. You will need these items for your verification visit. It is smart to mail your application materials with a return receipt requested. This way, you will have confirmation that the Council received them.

You should receive a call from a Council representative within ninety days of sending in your application. If this much time has elapsed without any word, you may want to call the Council to verify that your application materials were received and that you are in the queue for the verification visit.

Turn to chapter 6 on page 125 to read about the verification visit.

When the online application process becomes available, you can use this option instead of the traditional paper application. For additional information about the online application process, see pages 14–15.

CDA Process: Family Child Care

5

YOUR DECISION TO PROVIDE FAMILY CHILD CARE is an important one. Family child care comes in many forms, from a provider working on her own to a group of providers operating an organized agency of in-home programs. A person who chooses to provide family child care can specialize in part-time or full-time care, twenty-four-hour care, infant care, or care for mixed ages. Often, family child care providers decide on this type of care because they want to stay at home with their own children or they want the flexibility of providing the type of care they prefer. They sometimes have an assistant or two, depending on the number of children in their care.

Family child care is usually more informal and flexible than that found in center-based programs, and it provides a setting similar to what children would experience in their own homes. Also, family child care typically serves smaller groups of children, which offers more opportunities for individualized care and interaction. All in all, family child care comes in as many forms as there are family child care providers.

The typical family child care provider cares for a mixed-age group, with children between the ages of birth and five years, although she may care for school-age children for part of the day as well.

This type of care can be very challenging. The care provider must divide her time among many tasks and roles. She will cook, play, clean, teach, and socialize. She will need special skills and knowledge about the development of children at different ages to provide appropriate activities and care and to meet the children's individual needs. In addition, she will need skills in running her home business, including marketing and record keeping. A family child care program is often funded solely by the payments made to the provider by the parents, but many times additional funding comes from federal, state, or county programs or agencies in the form of subsidies, which requires yet additional bookkeeping and management skills.

In spite of the challenges and demands of the work, family child care is also very rewarding for those who choose to do it. These providers have the opportunity to form warm, loving relationships with young children who often remain in the program for a number of years prior to going to school and may even continue on an after-school basis thereafter. Family child care providers have the satisfaction of operating their programs in their own homes, often caring for their own children at the same time.

The CDA assessment system and Competency Standards for family child care were developed to evaluate family child care programs for quality and competent care. The standards outline the specific skills that a provider needs to meet the needs of the children, whether they are infants, toddlers, or preschoolers. The standards do not expect family child care programs to be set up and run like child care centers. They recognize the unique nature of family child care, with its flexible schedule and routines and the varied personalities and visions of the individuals who provide the care.

As you look over *The Child Development Associate Assessment System and Competency Standards for Family Child Care Providers* (Council for Professional Recognition 2006), you will see six Competency Goals on which you will be evaluated. In the process of working toward your credential, you will need to complete several tasks that at first glance may appear to be quite challenging. If you take them one step at a time, however, you will find the effort not only well within your capability but also very rewarding. Having completed or nearly completed the 120 clock hours of training, you are ready to begin the CDA process. Your Professional Resource File should now be set up and ready to fill with the Professional Resource Collection.

Assembling the Professional Resource Collection

You have already completed your autobiography, and it should be in the first section of your Professional Resource File. Next, type a label for the second divider page, whose tab you labeled "Competency Goal I." Type the label as follows:

> **COMPETENCY GOAL I**
> *To establish and maintain a safe,*
> *healthy learning environment*

Notice that the first line is capitalized and the second line is italicized. You will do the same. Place the label in the center of the second divider page, whose tab you labeled "Competency Goal I." Behind this second divider, insert four empty page protectors.

Now type a label to place on each of these page protectors. On the labels, type the numbered items listed under Competency Goal I. On the first label, for example, type the following, being sure to include the number:

> **1. Provide a summary of the legal requirements in your state regarding child abuse and neglect (including contact information for the appropriate agency) and also your program's policy regarding your responsibility to report child abuse and neglect.**

Place the label on the upper right corner of the first empty page protector. You now know instantly what goes into that page protector. You can probably find this information in your state child care licensing regulations or from your state child abuse prevention agency. Remember to include the phone number to call for information or to report abuse. Also, find out what the policy for reporting child abuse is for family child care programs in your state. Type this up after the previous information under a heading, such as "My Program's Policies for Reporting Child Abuse." Print all of this and insert it into the first page protector. Make sure you position the information on the paper so that the label on the page protector isn't covering it.

Even when you have put all the resources into the page protectors, keep the labels on them, as it makes the CDA representative's job much easier. She can see, without a doubt, that all seventeen items are there and that your file is complete.

The second page protector in this section will have a label typed as follows:

> **2. Include the current certificate of completion of a certified pediatric first-aid training course (that includes treatment for blocked airway and providing rescue breathing for infants and young children). Certification must have been within the past three years.**

Make sure your training was for pediatric first aid, *not* adult first aid! Do *not* include a copy of your CPR certificate unless it is combined with your first-aid certificate. It was not requested and the Council frowns on items being included in the Professional Resource File that were not asked for specifically.

You do not need to put the italicized words you see in parentheses (for example, *Cooperative Extension Service or Child Care Food Program*) on the label.

Now place this label on the top right corner of the second page protector. Make a copy of your first-aid certificate and insert it into this page protector.

The third page protector in this section will have a label typed as follows:

> **3. Use the Internet, the public library, or your program's professional library to obtain the name and contact information for an agency that supplies information on nutrition for children and/or nutrition education for families.**

Place this label on the third page protector. After you locate the requested information, type it, print it, and insert it into this page protector. The fourth page protector in this section will have a label typed as follows:

> **4. Provide a sample of your weekly plan that includes goals for children's learning and development, brief descriptions of planned learning experiences, and also accommodations for children with special needs (whether for children you currently serve or may serve in the future).**

You can use the weekly activity plan form you usually use in your program, perhaps enlarging it to accommodate the information that is required. Be sure to address all of the typical learning areas, such as art, language/literacy, circle, fine/gross motor, dramatic play, math, and science. In addition to listing the activities, you need to write learning goals for each activity, that is, what you expect the children to learn or how their development will be enhanced by doing the activities. You must also explain how each of your activities could be adapted to enable a child with special needs to participate. For an example of this, see the sample Individual Weekly Activity Plan for Infants on page 186 and the sample Weekly Activity Plans for Toddlers and Preschoolers on pages 188 and 189. You have now completed collecting resources for Competency Goal I and are ready to move on to Competency Goal II.

Make a label for the third divider page, whose tab you have labeled "Competency Goal II." This label should read as follows:

> **COMPETENCY GOAL II**
> *To advance physical and intellectual competence*

Place the label in the center of the divider page. Then place four page protectors behind this divider. Only the first page protector needs to be labeled. The label on the first page protector should read as follows:

> **5. Select four songs, fingerplays, word games, or poems that you can use to promote phonological awareness. Describe strategies to promote phonological awareness among children whose home language is other than English.**

Place this label on the top right corner of the first page protector. You can go to the library and look in the children's department to find what you need. Ask the librarian to see the teachers' books section. You can also search the Internet for these items.

Phonological awareness means hearing the sounds of letters and words. For young children, choosing songs, word games, and poems with an abundance of rhyming words and/or alliteration will help them in this area. *Alliteration* means the repetition of the same or similar consonant sounds at the beginning of words, as in "The tiny tiger took a tumble." Children whose home language is not English will benefit from similar activities, but teachers can also include activities in their native languages.

You can either type the items yourself or print examples from the Internet. Your explanation of strategies for promoting phonological awareness with English-language learners (ELL) should be typed on a separate page. Put these pages in the four page protectors, back to back.

Now, make a label for the next resource item you will put in your file, typing it as follows:

> **6. Describe nine learning experiences that promote physical, cognitive, and creative development—three for infants, three for toddlers, and three for preschoolers. Describe the goals, materials, and teaching strategies used.**

Add three more page protectors to this section, placing the label you have just made in the upper right corner of the first one.

Describe the nine activities, three for each of the age groups. For each activity, provide a title, a list of goals (what you want the children to do or learn), a list of materials needed, and the procedure for presenting the activity to children (step by step). Then explain how the activity promotes physical, cognitive, and creative development. It should look something like the following example for toddlers:

Activity for Toddlers

Title: Playdough Fun

Goals: Children will manipulate playdough using their hands and various utensils. They will use their language skills to talk about what they are experiencing and doing.

Materials: Playdough, trays, assorted wooden dowels, plastic spoons, child-sized table, and chairs

Procedure: Place playdough on trays with an assortment of wooden and plastic utensils. Give one tray to each child. Encourage the children to manipulate the playdough to create something of their own choosing. Encourage the children to talk about what they are doing and how the playdough looks and feels.

This activity supports physical development because the children use their hands to manipulate the playdough and utensils. They strengthen their small-motor skills while doing so.

This activity supports cognitive development because the children have opportunities to feel different textures, count pieces of playdough, learn different colors and shapes, and use language to talk about what they are doing.

This activity supports creative development because the children create something of their own choosing by manipulating the playdough any way they like.

Describe two more activities for toddlers, using this format. Next, using the same format, describe three activities appropriate for infants. Finally, describe three activities appropriate for preschoolers. You will have a total of nine activities. Type the three activities for each age group on separate pages. Place the pages back to back in the page protectors.

You are now finished collecting resources for Competency Goal II and are ready to move on to Competency Goal III. Make a label for the fourth divider page, whose tab you have labeled "Competency Goal III." This label should read as follows:

> **COMPETENCY GOAL III**
> *To support social and emotional development*
> *and to provide positive guidance*

Place the label in the center of the divider page. Then place three page protectors behind this divider. The label for the first page protector should read like this:

> **7. Provide the titles, authors, publishers, copyright dates, and short summaries of ten age-appropriate children's books *that you use* to support development of children's self-concept and self-esteem and to help children deal with life's challenges.**

Place this label on the first page protector. Go to the library and ask the children's librarian to help you find these books. Be sure to choose books that have copyright dates less than ten years old. Books that help children deal with life challenges, such as death, moving to a new home, starting a new school, or welcoming a new baby, are known as *bibliotherapy* or *therapeutic* books. Do *not* cut and paste information from an Internet bookstore. These are to be books you have actually used with the children in your program and with which you are very familiar. Type the information requested on one or two pages and insert them back to back into the first page protector.

Next, type a label for the second page protector as follows:

> **8. Use the Internet, the public library, or your program's professional library to obtain at least two resources designed to assist teachers in constructively dealing with children with challenging behaviors (such as aggressive behavior like hitting or biting, or shyness).**

Place this label on the second page protector. Again, the librarian at your local library will be able to help you find the books and information you need. These will not be children's materials; they will be books or articles for *teachers*. Be sure to list at least two resources. Type the information and insert it into this page protector.

The third page protector should be labeled as follows:

> **9. Provide the name and telephone number of
> an agency in the community where you work
> for making referrals to family counseling.**

Be sure the agency you select is located in the community where you work and not merely a website or an agency somewhere in your state. Type the information and insert it into this page protector. You are now finished collecting resources for Competency Goal III and are ready to move on to Competency Goal IV.

In the center of the fifth divider, whose tab you labeled "Competency Goal IV," place a label that reads like this:

> **COMPETENCY GOAL IV**
> *To establish positive and productive
> relationships with families*

Behind this divider page, put two page protectors. Label the first page protector as follows:

> **10. Find out where to obtain resources, materials,
> and translation services for families whose
> home language is other than English. Provide
> the agency name and contact information.**

Locate the name of the local agency, along with its address and phone number. Find the name(s) of someone at the agency to contact for information. Type this information and insert it into this page protector.

The second page protector should be labeled as follows:

> **11. Document your program's policies
> that specify parents' responsibilities and
> what the program does for parents.**

You may find this information in your center's parent handbook or orientation materials. It may be helpful to format the information this way:

What My Program Does for Parents

- Provides their children with a warm, loving, and safe place to play and learn

- Provides their children with nutritious snacks and meals

- Provides their children with trained and qualified caregivers

- Provides communication with and feedback to the children's families to build a strong relationship between the program and the children's homes

What Parents Can Do for My Program

- Respect the program's illness policy

- Pick up their children on time

- Provide a complete change of clothing in case of accidents

- Visit the family child care program and participate with their child or children whenever possible

example

Remember, these are provided only as examples. You must use the policies specific to your program.

You are now finished collecting resources for Competency Goal IV and are ready to move on to Competency Goal V.

In the center of the sixth divider, whose tab you labeled "Competency Goal V," place this label:

> **COMPETENCY GOAL V**
> *To ensure a well-run, purposeful program*
> *responsive to participant needs*

Behind this divider, place three page protectors. Type a label that reads as follows to place on the first one.

> **12. Provide three samples of record-keeping forms used in early childhood programs. Include an accident report, an emergency form, and a third form of your choice.**

Be sure to include the two types of forms that are specifically requested: the accident report and the emergency form. The third form could be a registration form, an attendance sign-in sheet, a field-trip permission form, or a daily report form. Put each requested form in a separate page protector. You have now completed collecting resources for Competency Goal V and are ready to move on to Competency Goal VI.

In the center of the seventh divider, whose tab you labeled "Competency Goal VI," place a label that reads:

> **COMPETENCY GOAL VI**
> *To maintain a commitment to professionalism*

Behind this divider, place several page protectors. You will type a label that reads as follows to place on the first one.

> **13. Use the Internet, the public library, or your program's professional library to obtain the name, address, and phone number of your state's agency that regulates child care centers and homes. Describe two important requirements related to your job responsibilities.**

Type only the name, address, and phone number of your state's child care regulating agency and place this page in the first page protector. Then go to the website listed below to look up the child care regulations for your particular state:

National Resource Center of Health and Safety in Child Care
http://nrckids.org/STATES/states.htm

Print out the section(s) that describes the qualification requirements for personnel (teachers, directors, and assistants). You will find this information in the regulations under "Staffing," "Personnel Policies," or something similar. Print only these particular sections for your file. In these sections, locate a listing of important requirements that are related to your own particular job responsibilities as a teacher, an assistant teacher, or a director and highlight them with a yellow highlighting marker. Now, put these regulations in page protectors.

Choose two of the highlighted requirements and type them on a separate page with this title: "Requirements Related to My Job Responsibilities." Put this in the first labeled page protector, in front of the regulations.

What if your state does not regulate family child care homes? If this is the case, you will not be able to find the information you need at the website indicated above. Review the accreditation standards of the National Association for Family Child Care on the Internet at www.nafcc.org. Look for the section(s) that describes the qualification requirements for family child care providers. Print only these particular sections for your file. In these sections, locate a listing of important requirements that are related to your own particular job responsibilities as a family child care provider and highlight them with a yellow highlighting marker. Now put these regulations in page protectors.

Choose two of the highlighted requirements and type them on a separate page with this title: "Requirements Related to My Job Responsibilities." Put this in the first labeled page protector, in front of the regulations.

Type a label for the next page protector that reads as follows:

> **14. Review the websites of two or three national early childhood associations (one with a local affiliate) to obtain information about membership, their resources, and how to order. Download at least two resources from the Internet that will enhance your work.**

These associations could include the National Association for the Education of Young Children (NAEYC, www.naeyc.org) or the National Association for Family Child Care (NAFCC, www .nafcc.org). Type the requested information about the two or three associations and place it in the page protector. Be sure to include information about becoming a member, the types of resources that are available for download or purchase from each website, and how a person can order them.

Now find two articles on one of the websites that relate to your work with children. On the NAEYC website (www.naeyc .org), you can access back issues of the journal *Young Children*, which has many articles from which to choose. Print two articles and put them back to back into page protectors.

The next page protector will be labeled as follows:

> **15. Obtain four pamphlets or articles designed to help parents understand how young children develop and learn. Articles must help parents understand development and learning of children ages birth to 5 years. At least one article must relate to guidance.**

Put each pamphlet or article in its own page protector. Only the first page protector needs to be labeled. You can find some pamphlets like this at a pediatrician's office, your local hospital, the health department, or perhaps the public library. Articles may also be downloaded from the Internet. Be sure the pamphlets or articles you choose are written primarily for parents and guardians and address topics about how children grow and learn during infancy through the preschool years (birth through age five). This could include information about stages of development and what to expect a child to be doing at specific ages. It would *not* include information about immunizations, dental or physical health, or safety. Remember that one of the pamphlets or articles has to be about guidance and that you have been asked to include four items. Do *not* include more or less than four!

The next page protector will be labeled as follows:

> **16. Locate an observation tool to use in recording information about children's behavior. One copy should be blank; the other one should be filled out as a sample of your observation of an individual child.**

Use a form you typically use in your work with children. If you do not have such a form, you can use the observation tool provided on page 188. It is for recording an anecdotal record. An anecdotal record is a type of observation tool. It is a short, written record based on observation of a child's behavior. You may put both copies (one blank and one filled out) back to back in the same page protector. *Do not include the child's name on the observation.*

The next page protector will be labeled as follows:

> **17. Obtain contact information for at least two agencies in the community that provide resources and services for children with disabilities.**

Find information on two or three agencies, which might include those that provide physical therapy, occupational therapy, speech therapy, or other developmental or learning services. In some communities, the local school district provides these services. Be sure these are local agencies that families enrolled in your program can access. Include the name of each agency, its address, its phone number, and name(s) of a person(s) who can be contacted for information. Type this information and insert it into this page protector.

If all of your page protectors are filled, the Professional Resource Collection section of your Professional Resource File is complete! Resist the temptation to add materials and information that were not specifically asked for in your blue book. This will not impress the Council representative. On the contrary, it will indicate your inability to follow instructions and may interfere with the representative's ability to sort through the resources to determine whether your file is complete.

That being said, this Professional Resource File does belong to you. The Council representative will look it over and check it for accuracy but will not keep it. The Professional Resource Collection will be a valuable source of reference to you as a professional. After you receive your CDA Credential, you can continue to add resources to the original collection for your own personal use.

You are now ready to work on the third and final portion of the Professional Resource File: Competency Goal Statements. This is the last tabbed section of your file.

Writing the Competency Goal Statements

The national Competency Standards are used to evaluate a CDA candidate's skills in working with young children. Six Competency Goals within these standards state general goals for caregiver performance. Under each of the Competency Goals are one or more Functional Areas, for a total of thirteen. The thirteen Functional Areas define more specifically the skills and behaviors you must perform to meet each of the Competency Goals.

Your task will be to rewrite, in *your own* words and with *your own* individual understanding, each of the thirteen Functional Area statements. Next, you will provide several very specific examples from your own work with young children, which will demonstrate your competency in each of the Functional Areas.

Refer to part 3 in your blue CDA book. There you will see the Competency Goals written with the Functional Area statements in blue boxes. Each Functional Area is further defined by a Developmental Context or explanation for each of the four age groups: young infants, mobile infants, toddlers, and preschoolers. Finally, you will see a listing of examples of caregiver competence for each of the Functional Areas included.

Find Competency Goal I. Notice that it has three Functional Areas: Safe, Healthy, and Learning Environment. Begin writing your first Competency Goal Statement by typing exactly what you see written, with the first line in bold print and the second line in italics:

Competency Goal I
To establish and maintain a safe, healthy learning environment

Functional Area 1: Safe

Now, instead of writing what you see for Functional Area 1 in your book, you will need to rewrite it in *your own* words. Instead of writing "Candidate provides a safe environment to prevent and reduce injuries," you will personalize this statement in your own words. For some ideas on doing this, read the Developmental Context section under the Functional Area. Here are two examples of what you might write:

example   I make sure to provide a setting that promotes safety and minimizes the risk of injuries.

example   Safety is a main priority in the environment I provide for the children in my care. I make every effort to prevent injuries and accidents.

You can see that I've included all the main ideas of the Council's version but in my own words. Now write *your own* version. Do not use the word *will* in the statement, because this is not something you *will* be doing, but rather something you are doing right now. So if this were *my* Competency Goal Statement, it would look like this so far:

example

Competency Goal I
*To establish and maintain a safe,
healthy learning environment*

Functional Area 1: Safe

Safety is a main priority in the environment that I provide for the children in my care. I make every effort to prevent injuries and accidents.

You will now give *specific* examples of things *you* do in *your* program to satisfy this goal. If you look in your blue book, you will see a list of examples. You may *not* copy these examples. They are meant to give you ideas for writing your own. Also, they are much too general in nature. You should write examples that are specific to your own work with young children in your program. You will give two examples for each of the three age groups: infants (either young infants from birth through eight months or mobile infants from nine through seventeen months), toddlers, and preschoolers.

One of the general examples given in the book is "Does not give food to children that might cause choking." I may do things in my program to prevent children from choking, too, but what specifically? After thinking about it, I make a heading:

Infants

Then I write a specific example of how I anticipate and plan to avoid choking situations with infants:

I do this by

- Cutting finger foods into very small pieces when the children begin to feed themselves so the pieces can be swallowed easily.

example

I will write one more example of something I do to keep infants safe. Now I will make another heading:

Toddlers

I will write two specific examples of how I keep toddlers safe. Then I make a third heading:

Preschoolers

I write two specific examples of how I keep preschoolers safe. Now my Competency Goal Statement looks like this:

example

Competency Goal I
*To establish and maintain a safe,
healthy learning environment*

Functional Area 1: Safe

Safety is a main priority in the environment that I provide for the children in my care. I make every effort to prevent injuries and accidents.

Infants

I do this by

- Cutting finger foods into very small pieces when the children begin to feed themselves so the pieces can be swallowed easily.
- *(Another example).*

Toddlers

I do this by

- *(An example).*
- *(Another example).*

Preschoolers

I do this by

- *(An example).*
- *(Another example).*

After writing your own examples, you are ready to begin your Competency Goal Statement for Functional Area 2. Leave a few spaces, and write:

Functional Area 2: Healthy

Look at the statement written for Functional Area 2 in your book. Rewrite it in *your own* words, looking at the Developmental Context for ideas. I might write something like this:

example

> I encourage proper nutrition and good health habits every day by modeling these behaviors and providing an environment that promotes them and where risk of illness is reduced.

You try writing it in *your own* words. After you do, type "I do this by."

You may now give some *specific* examples of things *you* do in *your* program to satisfy this goal. Do *not* copy the examples provided in your book, but do gain some ideas from them. One of the examples in the book reads, "Cleans play areas and materials daily." Here is a specific example I might write for infants:

example

> At the end of each day, I wash all toys that have been mouthed by the children in warm, soapy water. Those items that cannot be washed in the sink are sanitized with a safe, nontoxic spray and left to air-dry.

Under Functional Area 2: Healthy, you need to write two specific examples of *your own* under each of the three age groups—infants, toddlers, and preschoolers—using the format suggested previously.

When you finish your examples, you will be ready to begin your Competency Goal Statement for Functional Area 3. Leave a few spaces and write this:

Functional Area 3: Learning Environment

Look at the statement written for Functional Area 3 in your book. Rewrite it in *your own* words, looking at the Developmental Context for ideas. I might write something like this:

example

> The learning environment I provide encourages children to feel comfortable, to be curious, to explore, and to learn. This is done through interesting activities, materials, and opportunities for socialization.

You try writing it in *your own* words. After you do, type "I do this by."

Now you are ready to write *specific* examples of how *you* satisfy this goal in *your* program. Look at the samples given in the book, using them for ideas. Again make three headings—one for infants, one for toddlers, and one for preschoolers—providing two examples for each. Here is a sample of a specific example for toddlers:

> I put all the children's toys in open bins that are labeled with pictures. They are stored on low, open shelves so the children have easy access to them and quickly learn how to put the toys away themselves.

example

After writing your examples for this Functional Area, you are finished with Competency Goal I.

The writing you have done for this Competency Goal must add up to between 200 and 500 words. Count only the words in the Functional Area statements and the examples under each of them. Please be sure to do a word count on your computer to be certain you are within this word-count range, as the Council is very particular about this. It is better to be closer to 500 words, because a thorough explanation of your competency is better than one that is too short and incomplete. That said, you should not go over 500 words, because the Council sees this as a failure to follow instructions and you will lose points. If your word count is well under 500 words, add additional examples under the Functional Areas. If you have more than 500 words, take out a couple of examples.

Now you are ready to go on to Competency Goal II. This Competency Goal has four Functional Areas: Physical, Cognitive, Communication, and Creative.

Begin Competency Goal II on a new page by copying exactly what you see written, with the first line in bold print and the second line in italics:

Competency Goal II
To advance physical and intellectual competence

Functional Area 4: Physical

Now, rewrite what you see written for Functional Area 4. It should be in *your own* words. Read the Developmental Context for ideas. I might write something like this:

> In my program, children have daily opportunities, both indoors and outdoors, to participate in activities that enhance their physical development.

example

You try writing it in *your own* words. After you do, type "I do this by."

Now give two *specific* examples for each of the three age groups of how *you* meet this goal in *your* program. Think of specific examples that encourage small- and large-motor development. Look at the examples for ideas, but do *not* copy them. Here is a sample of a specific example:

example

Infants

I do this by

- Placing the infants on their tummies on a firm, carpeted surface so they can lift up and strengthen their upper bodies several times a day. I provide interesting, colorful toys with moving parts to encourage them to reach and move.

Write two examples of your own for infants. Then write two examples for toddlers and two for preschoolers.

When you have finished writing your examples, you are ready to go on to Functional Area 5. Leave a few spaces and type this heading:

Functional Area 5: Cognitive

Look at the statement written for Functional Area 5. Write that statement in *your own* words. Read the Developmental Context for ideas. I might write something like this:

example

I feel it is important for children to exercise their curiosity and have opportunities to problem solve, so I provide an environment and activities that allow for discovery and exploration.

Now you write it in *your own* words. After you do, type "I do this by."

Write six *specific* examples of how *you* satisfy this goal in *your* program, two for each of the three age groups: infants, toddlers, and preschoolers. Look at the samples given in your book for ideas, but do *not* copy them. Here is a sample of a specific example:

example

Infants

I do this by

- Sometimes placing a colorful toy under the edge of a blanket while the children watch and asking them where it went. Then I lift it off and say, "Surprise!" They love this game and are learning the concept of object permanence.

Write two examples of your own for infants. Then write two examples for toddlers and two for preschoolers. When you have finished writing your examples, you are ready to go on to Functional Area 6. Leave a few spaces and type this:

Functional Area 6: Communication

Look at the statement written for Functional Area 6. Rewrite it in your own words. Read the Developmental Context for ideas. I may write something like this:

> I encourage children to develop verbal and nonverbal skills by offering many opportunities for them to express themselves, to listen, and to interact with adults and each other.

example

You write it in *your own* words. After you do, type "I do this by."

Now write *specific* examples of how *you* satisfy this goal in *your* program, two for each of the three age groups: infants, toddlers, and preschoolers. Look at the samples given in your book for ideas, but do *not* copy them. Here is a sample of a specific example:

Preschoolers

example

I do this by

• Always sitting at the table with the children at mealtimes. I initiate and encourage conversation by asking open-ended questions. Sometimes we tell jokes or funny stories. Everyone enjoys this time together.

Write two examples of your own for preschoolers. Then write two examples for infants and two for toddlers. When you have finished writing your examples, you are ready to go on to Functional Area 7. Leave a few spaces and type this:

Functional Area 7: Creative

Look at the statement written for Functional Area 7. You are going to rewrite it in *your own* words. Read the Developmental Context for ideas. I may write something like this:

> In my program, children have many opportunities to express themselves creatively through the materials, activities, and props I provide.

example

You try writing it in *your own* words. After you do, type "I do this by."

You will now write about how *you* satisfy this goal in *your* program, providing two *specific* examples for each of the three age groups: infants, toddlers, and preschoolers. You may look at the samples given in your book for ideas, but do *not* copy them. Here is a sample of a specific example:

example

Infants

I do this by

- Playing recordings of music with different tempos and rhythms. I hold the children, and we move and sway to the music. I encourage them to move their arms, legs, and hands.

Write two examples of your own for infants. Then write two examples for toddlers and two for preschoolers. After writing your examples, you will be finished with Competency Goal II. Check your word count to be sure it is near 500 words, but not more than that! You are now ready to begin Competency Goal III. Start a new page. Begin Competency Goal III by copying exactly what you see written:

Competency Goal III
*To support social and emotional development
and to provide positive guidance*

Functional Area 8: Self

Look at the statement written for Functional Area 8. Rewrite it in *your own* words. Read the Developmental Context for ideas. I may write something like this:

example

I provide opportunities for children to feel successful, to feel proud of themselves, and to do things independently. In my program, children feel safe, secure, and loved.

You try writing it in *your own* words. After you do, type "I do this by."

Now write *specific* examples of how *you* satisfy this goal in *your* program, two for each of the three age groups: infants, toddlers, and preschoolers. Look at the samples given in your book for ideas, but do *not* copy them. Here is a sample of a specific example:

example

Toddlers

I do this by

- Giving each child warm hugs "just because" many times during the day. Now they are not only spontaneously hugging me, but each other as well!

Write two examples of your own for toddlers. Then write two examples for infants and two for preschoolers. When you have finished writing your examples, you are ready to go on to Functional Area 9. Leave a few spaces and type the following:

Functional Area 9: Social

Look at the statement written for Functional Area 9. You are going to rewrite it in *your own* words. Read the Developmental Context for ideas. I may write something like this:

> The children in my program are given opportunities to learn cooperation and social interaction. They are encouraged to communicate and to get along with each other.

example

You try writing it in *your own* words. Then type "I do this by."

Now write *specific* examples of how *you* satisfy this goal in *your* program, two for each of the three age groups: infants, toddlers, and preschoolers. Look at the samples given in your book for ideas, but do *not* copy them. Here is a sample of a specific example:

Infants

example

I do this by

- Providing duplicates of our favorite toys, such as the fire truck and the pop-up boxes, so one child doesn't have to wait for another child to finish playing and the children don't get into conflicts over one toy.

Write two examples of your own for infants. Then write two examples for toddlers and two for preschoolers. When you have finished writing your examples, you are ready to go on to Functional Area 10. Leave a few spaces and type this:

Functional Area 10: Guidance

Look at the statement written for Functional Area 10. You are going to rewrite it in *your own* words. Read the Developmental Context for ideas. I may write something like this:

> I help children learn to be self-disciplined through support, consistency, and positive role-modeling.

example

You try writing it in *your own* words. Then type "I do this by."

Now write *specific* examples of how *you* satisfy this goal in *your* program, two for each of the three age groups: infants, toddlers, and preschoolers. Look at the samples given in your book for ideas, but do *not* copy them. Here is a sample of a specific example:

Infants

example

I do this by

- Responding immediately to an infant when he or she wakes and begins to fuss after a nap. This helps the child learn to trust me.

Write two examples of your own for infants. Then write two examples for toddlers and two for preschoolers. After writing your examples, you will be finished with Competency Goal III. Check your word count to be sure it is near 500 words, but not more than that! You are ready to go on to Competency Goal IV. Start a new page. Begin Competency Goal IV by copying exactly what you see written, with the first line in bold type and the line below it in italics:

Competency Goal IV
*To establish positive and productive
relationships with families*

Functional Area 11: Families

Look at the statement written for Functional Area 11. You are going to rewrite it in *your own* words. Read the Developmental Context for ideas. I may write something like this:

example
> I encourage the children's families to get involved in our activities whenever possible. I encourage and support a close relationship between home and school.

You try writing it in *your own* words. Then type "I do this by."
Now write *specific* examples of how *you* satisfy this goal in *your* program, two for each of the three age groups: infants, toddlers, and preschoolers. Look at the samples given in your book for ideas, but do *not* copy them. Here is a sample of a specific example:

example
Infants

I do this by

• Sending home a daily, personalized sheet about each infant, describing feeding times and amounts eaten, diapering information, how we played, what the child enjoyed, and a suggestion or two for the families so they can stimulate development at home.

Write two examples of your own for infants. Then write two examples for toddlers and two for preschoolers. When you have finished writing your examples, you are ready to go on to Competency Goal V. Start a new page. Begin Competency Goal V by copying what you see written, with the first line in bold type and the line below it in italics:

Competency Goal V
*To ensure a well-run, purposeful program
responsive to participant needs*

Look at the statement written for Functional Area 12. You are going to rewrite it in *your own* words. Read the Developmental Context for ideas. I may write something like this:

> I maintain a well-run program by being organized and observant, keeping accurate records, and developing long- and short-term plans.

You try writing it in *your own* words. Then type "I do this by."

Write *specific* examples of how *you* satisfy this goal in *your* program. You may look at the samples given in your book for ideas, but do *not* copy them. Here is a sample of a specific, detailed example:

> I do this by
>
> • Keeping a small spiral notebook in my pocket. In it, I record anecdotal notes on the children as they play, try new things, master skills, and interact with each other. I share these notes with the parents and guardians during conferences and use them for planning developmentally appropriate activities for the children.

You will notice that this sample is rather wordy. Since Competency Goal V has only one Functional Area, your examples can go into greater detail. You will also need to include at least six or seven examples, instead of three, to bring the word count near 500 words. After writing your own six or seven examples, you will be finished with Competency Goal V. Make sure the word count for this Competency Goal is near 500 words. You are now ready to go on to Competency Goal VI. Start a new page. You will begin Competency Goal VI by copying exactly what you see written, with the first line in bold type and the line below it in italics:

Competency Goal VI
To maintain a commitment to professionalism

Functional Area 13: Professionalism

Look at the statement written for Functional Area 13. You are going to rewrite it in *your own* words. Read the Developmental Context for ideas. I may write something like this:

> I consider myself a professional and, as such, constantly seek additional education in child development and developmentally appropriate practice. I often attend

---

example

For Functional Area 12: Program Management and Functional Area 13: Professional Development, you will not need to provide separate examples for each of the three age groups (infants, toddlers, and preschoolers) as you did for Functional Areas 1 through 11. These final two Functional Areas refer to things you do to maintain a quality program and to increase your own professionalism, which affect all of the age groups as a whole.

---

example

workshops offered in my community as well as attend early childhood conferences. I aim to do the best I possibly can for the children and families in my program.

You try writing it in *your own* words. Then type "I do this by."

You will now write six or seven *specific* examples of how *you* satisfy this goal in *your* program. You may look at the samples given in your book for ideas, but do *not* copy them. Here is a sample of two specific examples:

example

I do this by

- Being a member of NAEYC and also of my local chapter. I work on the membership committee and encourage others to join and support young children through this organization.

- Keeping all information about the children in my class and about their families confidential. I do not discuss personal information that parents may share with me, nor do I compare one child with another in front of parents, guardians, or anyone else. I want the parents and guardians in my program to feel they can come to me with questions or concerns without worrying about the information being shared with others. By so doing, I can build strong connections between home and school for the benefit of the children.

When you finish writing your six or seven specific examples for this Functional Area, you will be finished with Competency Goal VI. Check your word count to be sure it is near 500 words.

Place all six of your completed Competency Goal Statements in your Professional Resource File, behind the divider whose tab is labeled "Competency Goal Statements." You might want to put these sheets into page protectors, but before you do, make copies of them to give to the Council representative during your verification visit. Place these copies into the file folder or pocket folder where you have already placed a copy of your autobiography.

Congratulations! Your Professional Resource File is complete.

Preparing for the Assessment Observation by the CDA Advisor

The next step in your CDA process is to prepare for the assessment observation by your CDA advisor. With any luck, you have been able to locate an advisor of your own choosing, or you have contacted the Council for a listing of registered CDA advisors in your area.

The CDA advisor is the only person who will visit and observe you working with young children in your program. The Council representative, on the other hand, will meet with a candidate only to conduct the verification visit. She will *not* be observing.

Being prepared for your advisor's visit(s) is important. As soon as you receive your CDA application packet, it is a good idea to make a photocopy of the CDA Assessment Observation Instrument booklet. It is the stapled booklet with a yellow cover. Use it to do a self-study on your work with the children in your classroom, as well as on the classroom environment, before your advisor comes out to do an observation.

Looking at the CDA Assessment Observation Instrument booklet, notice that each item is to be rated 3, 2, or 1. A rating of 3 means you can be observed complying with this item *most* of the time. A rating of 2 means you can be observed complying with this item *sometimes*. A rating of 1 means you can be observed *rarely* complying with this item.

As you go through your photocopied booklet and rate yourself, if you note any items rated below a 3, write some notes in the margin to yourself about what is not up to par and how you plan to remedy the situation. Do not underestimate the importance of doing this self-study. It is important that you become familiar with the things your advisor will be looking for and on which you will be rated. You should come to work the day of your advisor's visit having prepared your classroom and yourself for a successful observation.

You need to be observed while working as a *primary caregiver* in a family child care program that meets at least the minimum requirements for state and/or local licensing or registration of family child care homes. In areas where no regulation of family child care homes exists, providers may be assessed without this documentation. You need to be working with a group of at least three children, all of whom are from birth through five years old. Your advisor will also assess your classroom environment based on national CDA standards.

Ideally, the advisor visits you at least once prior to conducting the official assessment observation. This will be an informal visit. She will look around, watch you in action with the children, and take notes. Afterward, she will share her observations, indicate problem areas, and suggest ways of improving.

The final observation will be a formal one and your advisor will not be able to offer any feedback to you about it. Your advisor will record her assessments, notes, and ratings in the yellow CDA Assessment Observation Instrument booklet. The items to be rated are arranged according to the Competency Goals and Functional Areas.

It will not be possible for the advisor to observe *all* of the items on the Assessment Observation Instrument. Perhaps she will not be at your family child care home at snacktime so she won't see the procedures you follow. In such a case, she will ask you about these items that were not observed and record your answers and comments. The formal observation may take as long as three hours.

After completing the observation of your work, your advisor will return the Assessment Observation Instrument booklet to you, sealed in an envelope. It must *remain sealed* to be given to the Council representative when she visits you. If the seal on this Assessment Observation Instrument booklet is broken, the Council will not accept it. The assessment observation will have to be repeated, a new Assessment Observation Instrument booklet completed, and the verification visit rescheduled for a future date. All of this will cause an unnecessary delay in the award of your credential, perhaps by several months, so remember to simply keep the Assessment Observation Instrument booklet sealed in the envelope!

As you worked to complete your six Competency Goal Statements, you read over the listing of examples under each Functional Area in the blue CDA book. These examples represent the criteria that define a successful CDA candidate. You also completed a self-study based on the items in the CDA Assessment Observation Instrument, as previously suggested. In addition to these valuable steps in preparing for your assessment observation, you will benefit from reading over some additional program tips based on the CDA Competency Standards.

Program Tips

The areas in your room should be safe and free from hazards. Good health should be promoted.

- Sharp corners should be covered.

- Flimsy shelving and furniture should be removed.

- Electrical cords should be wound up and out of reach.

- Miniblind cords should be secured to the tops of windows.

- Small items that could be ingested should not be left out on tables or on the floor.

- Household cleaning supplies, prescription medications, and other drugs should be kept secured and locked, and houseplants should be kept out of reach.

- Precautions should be taken when the stove is in use and safety latches should be used on drawers and cabinets.

- Area rugs should be secured to the floor to prevent tripping.

- Caregivers should wash their hands before handling food, after assisting children in the restroom, and after wiping noses.

- Close supervision should be maintained at all times. Care providers should always position themselves so they have full view of the room and should never turn their backs on the children.

- The room should be generally clean and tidy.

- Accommodations should be made for different developmental stages by, for example, using safety gates and outlet covers.

- Restrooms should be sanitized daily. Liquid soap and disposable towels should be available for the children's use.

- Covered, plastic-lined trash cans should be available.

- Children should have separate storage for their own belongings.

- A simple escape route should be posted near the door.

- A chart of CPR and first-aid procedures should be posted.

- There should be a first-aid kit readily available. If it is in a cabinet, the outside of the cabinet should be labeled "First Aid" to indicate where it is located.

- At least one fully charged fire extinguisher should be available nearby, and you should be trained in its use.

- Functioning smoke detectors should be installed.

- Good nutrition should be the focus of snacks and meals served. Processed foods and junk foods should not be served. Fruit juice, water, or milk should be the only beverage choices, no Kool-Aid or soda. Adults should not consume sodas or junk foods around the children.

- When the children eat, the care providers should sit at the tables with them, modeling good table manners, encouraging them to try new foods, and engaging them in pleasant conversation.

- Include the children, when possible, in the preparation of food for the group or in helping with simple household chores.

The area(s) of your home designated for child care should be set up specifically for children.

- Provide a good variety of materials and toys that are easily accessible to the children and will encourage them to put items away themselves.

- Take advantage of neighborhood opportunities, such as parks, a public library, gardens, snowy hills, or friendly neighbors.

- There should be child-sized furniture for the children. This would include tables and chairs.

- Organize play areas within the home so that similar activities are placed adjacent to each other, younger children have protected areas in which to play, and older children can use materials suited to their developmental levels without interruption.

- There should be opportunities for dramatic play. You may have a child-sized kitchen set, doll beds, dolls, dress-up clothes, and other props. Safe household items should be available, such as pots, pans, lids, and plastic cups.

- There should be a set of building blocks, preferably wood unit blocks, available to the children. The block area should include props, such as small people or animal figures, to encourage creative play.

- Some kind of book corner or shelves should include children's books that the children can look at whenever they like. These books may be from your own collection or borrowed weekly from the public library. Other literacy materials should be available as the children show readiness for them, such as child-sized pencils, various types of papers, markers, and washable stamp pads and stamps.

- The environment should be literacy rich. The items in the room should be labeled wherever possible (for example, a small sign on the door that reads "door").

- Children should be read to frequently every day.

- Cultural diversity should be promoted through multiethnic and multiracial dolls and pretend foods of other cultures for dramatic play, posters reflecting differences, and a collection of multicultural children's books.

- Both boys and girls should have opportunities and be encouraged to play in all areas, free from gender bias.

- Adaptations and accommodations should be made for children with special needs.

- There should be opportunities for older and younger children to play together.

There should be opportunities for both large- and small-motor development, as well as cognitive development.

- Age-appropriate manipulatives, puzzles, stacking and sorting toys, interlocking blocks, playdough, and simple, homemade materials to play with should be available.

- There should be a safe place for the children to engage in outdoor play with age-appropriate equipment, such as a climber, swings, a slide, riding toys, and balls.

- Alternate indoor, large-motor activities should be available in case of inclement weather.

Children should have opportunities for creative activities on a daily basis, using creative arts materials.

- Paint, crayons, colored chalk, and markers should be readily available.

- Open-ended process art activities, such as collage, free-form cutting and pasting, or fingerpainting should be offered. No crafts or coloring book pages should be used.

Children should have the opportunity to learn through play with hands-on activities.

- Learning about colors, for example, should be done by manipulating real items of different colors, not by drill or flash cards.

- Learning shapes and numbers should be done through tactile experiences or games, not through flash cards or drills.

- There should be opportunities for many sensory activities, such as cooking, using playdough, handling different textures, and practicing visual discrimination.

- Absolutely no worksheets should be used.

- There should be a variety of age-appropriate toys, materials, and activities.

- Discovery, exploration, and problem solving should be encouraged.

- Children's varied learning styles should be respected and supported by individualizing the activities.

Children should have regular, short, age-appropriate group or circle activities as well as individual interactions that encourage socialization between adults and children and among the children themselves.

- Games should be played.

- Very limited use of videos or television is acceptable.

- Movement activities with or without props or music should be provided.

- Stories should be read on a regular basis.

- Both caregivers and children should have opportunities to engage in storytelling.

- Flannelboard stories should be used to provide variety in the presentation of books.

- Fingerplays should be introduced.

- Music should be incorporated into the daily schedule.

- Group activities should not include any type of drills, flash cards, or memorization.

Children should have predictable routines, although daily activities may be flexible to suit the children's needs or interests.

- Greet each child and adult individually upon arrival.

- Use songs and games to ease transitions from one activity to the next, giving children ample notice when a change is about to occur.

- Have an activity planned for children who finish/transition early, so they do not have to wait for the rest of the group.

- Have daily lesson plans and the materials to carry them out on hand when needed.

Children should be given the opportunity to learn self-discipline in positive, supportive ways.

- Establish a few simple rules with the children. Post them, using pictures to convey the ideas. The rules should be stated in *positive* terms, for example, "Use walking feet," rather than "Don't run."

- Use redirection whenever possible.

- Provide logical and natural consequences for misbehavior.

- Encourage children to use words to convey their feelings.

- Model cooperation, sharing, and proper behavior.

- Use a normal voice with the children. Never shout.

- Show ample affection to each child.

- Expect children to help maintain the environment by having them help pick up toys and clean up messes.

- Give children the opportunity to problem solve with each other. Don't be too eager to step in.

- Anticipate problems before they happen, if possible, by being observant.

Interact and play with the children indoors and outdoors.

- Play along with the children whenever possible and involve them in household activities and routines.

- Be a good listener. Ask lots of open-ended questions and be patient with children as they speak. Spend time talking with each child every day.

Develop a partnership with the families in your program.

- Communicate regularly when family members drop off or pick up their children.

- Invite family members to become involved in your program.

- Maintain a parent bulletin board with upcoming activities, parenting tips, child development information, and community resources available to them.

Maintain a well-run, organized program.

- Keep up-to-date health and emergency information files on each child in your care.

- Develop a brochure or leaflet for parents and guardians, outlining your program's policies, goals, services offered, and mission statement.

- Take anecdotal notes on each child.

- Keep a portfolio for each child that contains these anecdotal notes, samples of the child's art, and other evidence of skill development that can be shared with parents and guardians.

Maintain a commitment to professionalism.

- Join a national or local early childhood organization.

- Observe a strict policy of confidentiality with the families in your program.

- Continue to improve your skills by attending workshops or classes.

- Network with other family child care providers for support and exchange of program ideas and resources.

After your advisor has completed your assessment observation and all of your other documentation has been completed, you are ready to submit the Direct Assessment Application form. This indicates to the Council that you are ready for your verification visit.

Completing and Submitting the Direct Assessment Application Form

Does it matter when I send in my application?

No. Applications are now accepted on a rolling basis, which means there are no longer quarterly submission deadlines. Your verification visit will occur within ninety days of the Council receiving your application. Of course, this is assuming you completed the application correctly and included all of the necessary documentation. It is important to remember that your Parent Opinion Questionnaires and the Assessment Observation Instrument cannot be dated more than six months prior to the time the application form is sent in.

The Direct Assessment Application form came with your application packet, and it can be downloaded from the Council's website. A sample of this form has been provided on page 198.

The form is divided into eight sections. Section 1, Type of Assessment, is where you will check "Family Child Care." You will not need to check "Monolingual" or "Bilingual" unless applicable. Under section 2, Type of Program, check "Family Child Care."

Section 3 asks for your personal information. Section 4, Payment, asks you to indicate how the Direct Assessment fee is being paid, either directly by you or through an agency. If you are paying the fee yourself, you will need to send a check or money order with the application form.

In section 5, you are asked for a breakdown of your training hours into specific content areas with at least ten clock hours per area:

1. Planning a safe, healthy learning environment

2. Steps to advance children's physical and intellectual development

3. Positive ways to support children's social and emotional development

4. Strategies to establish productive relationships with families

5. Strategies to manage an effective program operation

6. Maintaining a commitment to professionalism

7. Observing and recording children's behavior

8. Principles of child development and learning

Put the number of clock hours of training you have had in each of these eight subject areas in the boxes after the descriptions. Often you can ask the institution or agency where you received this training to help you do this. Sometimes a course syllabus or outline of topics covered in a class or training session is also helpful. You can also look at the listing of subject areas with examples that is provided in appendix A on page 179.

You need to acquire verification of the training sessions for courses you have taken. This can be in the form of a certificate, an official letter on letterhead, or a transcript. The verification must also indicate the content area(s) of the training, the number of clock hours, and the name and address of the training institution or agency, and include an authorized signature. If your training occurred at several venues, you need this verification from each of them. Remember, the Council does not accept training hours obtained from consultants or conference workshops. Also in section 5, on the upper right, you are asked whether you received college credits for any of your training hours and, if so, how many. This item is easy to overlook, so be sure to complete it.

Section 6 asks you to verify certain things by making check marks next to each statement. One of the questions asks you to indicate that you have read the NAEYC Code of Ethical Conduct. This code provides a guide for conduct, practice, and ethical responsibility for early care and education providers. You received a copy of this document in the application packet. If you do not have a copy, you can download one from the NAEYC website (www.naeyc.org). Other questions in this section ask whether you have distributed and collected the Parent Opinion Questionnaires, been observed by your advisor, and completed your Professional Resource File. You may not send in your application until you can check off these items as being completed.

If you have applied to the Council for any type of waiver, indicate this by checking the last box and attaching your Waiver Request form to the application. If you have applied for either a bilingual or monolingual assessment, fill in the last two items of section 6. Finally, sign and date the form, as indicated.

If you own and operate the family child care program, complete section 7 yourself. Otherwise it must be completed by the person who is the owner or director. Your CDA advisor will complete section 8, indicating the date of the formal observation, noting the children's ages and program setting, and verifying that the CDA Assessment Observation Instrument was completed, put into a sealed envelope, and given to you.

When this form has been completed, retain the bottom copy for yourself. Then mail the application in with the designated payment, verification of training (including transcripts), description of the content of the training you had, and verification from your license that you have at least 480 hours working with children ages birth through five years within the past five years. These are the *only* items that are to be sent with the application form. Do *not* send your Professional Resource File, Competency Goal Statements, autobiography, or Parent Opinion Questionnaires to the Council. You will need these items for your verification visit. It is smart to mail your application materials with a return receipt requested. This way, you will have confirmation that the Council received them.

You should receive a call from a Council representative within ninety days of sending in your application. If this much time has elapsed without any word, you may want to call the Council to verify that your application materials were received and that you are in the queue for the verification visit.

When the online application process becomes available, you can use this option instead of the traditional paper application. For additional information about the online application process, see pages 14–15.

Continue to chapter 6 for information on the verification visit.

The Verification Visit 6

What to Expect

After you've submitted the application form along with the fee and proof of your training, several weeks may pass before your verification visit is scheduled. The Council will need to look over and approve your application materials. The Council will select a Council representative in your area to conduct the visit. This selection is based on a Council representative's expertise in the setting, the age-level endorsement, and the specialization of the candidate the representative will be assessing. All Council representatives have been trained to conduct assessments in center-based preschool settings, but only Council representatives who have received specialized training will be assigned to family child care, infant/toddler, home visitor, bilingual assessments, or special education.

If more than a month has elapsed with no word, you can call the Council to ask whether your application materials were received and you are in the queue for the verification visit.

The Council representative will contact you at least twice. The first time will be to introduce herself and answer any questions you may have about the verification visit procedures. She will ask you to verify your setting (center-based or family child care) and the color of the book you used to prepare for your assessment (green for preschool, yellow for infant/toddler, or blue for family child care). The representative will also ask how old the children in your group were when your advisor conducted your assessment observation, as well as how many children were in the group. If you have requested a bilingual assessment, the representative will ask you to identify your preferred language and may speak to you in that language and in English to determine whether you are indeed bilingual.

The Council representative will go through a checklist with you during this first call to be sure you have all of the required materials ready to bring along to the verification visit including these items:

- Your completed Parent Opinion Questionnaires in a sealed envelope with the number distributed and the number collected written on the front. The representative will also make sure the questionnaires are dated within six months of your application submission.

- The CDA Assessment Observation Instrument booklet that was completed by your advisor, placed in a sealed envelope. It, too, must be dated within six months of your application submission. (If you are a center-based infant/toddler care provider, your advisor will also have included the Supplemental Observation form in the same sealed envelope.)

- Your completed Professional Resource File which includes these items:

  o Autobiography

  o Six Competency Goal Statements

  o Professional Resource Collection with seventeen items

- Separate copies of your autobiography and the six Competency Goal Statements.

- Your *original* first-aid certificate. (You need a copy of this certificate in your Professional Resource File only until the day of your verification visit, and then you can replace it with the original.)

- A photo ID (a driver's license, for example).

Next, the Council representative will arrange with you a date, place, and time for the verification visit. If you are in a center-based program, the assessment may be held at your center. It must be in a quiet area that has a door and adult-sized chairs and tables. The representative will want you to provide the phone number, address, and detailed directions to your center so she can be sure to arrive at the scheduled time without undue delays. She will also contact your center director to confirm permission to conduct the assessment at the center. By signing your application form, the director already granted permission, so this is only an act of courtesy.

If an acceptable meeting space is not available at your center, a conference room at a public library or community center would be a good alternative. If you have arranged for the assessment to take place at an alternate site, the Council representative will still call your director to pass along this information. The representative will also inform the director that the Council requires candidates to keep all assessment information confidential, which will preclude any questions being asked of you at work after your verification visit.

You are not to discuss your verification visit with anyone, including your employer, which is a good policy. That way you can steer clear of uncomfortable situations. If someone presses you for information about "how you did," simply remind them of the Council's confidentiality policy.

If you are a family child care provider, the assessment may *not* be in your own home or in anyone else's home. An alternate site, such as a public library or community center, needs to be arranged.

The Council representative will call you a second time to confirm the date, time, and location of the verification visit and to remind you to bring along a picture ID. Many times, the Council representative will schedule several candidates for a verification visit at the same place, date, and time. They may be individuals you work with in your program or they may be candidates from other programs.

A Council representative can have a number of candidates complete the Early Childhood Studies Review exam at the same time and can look over their materials; however, the representative is allowed to conduct only *three* oral interviews on one particular day. So if more than three candidates are scheduled for the same verification visit, you will all take the exam while the representative checks over your Professional Resource Files, autobiographies, Competency Goal Statements, Parent Opinion Questionnaires, and Assessment Observation Instrument booklets. On that particular day, though, only three of you will have an oral interview. The others will need to have their oral interviews scheduled for another date within three weeks.

If, for some reason, when you arrive at your verification visit, the Council representative says she will conduct more than three interviews on that day, ask for your oral interview to be scheduled on a future date. Then when you get home, call the Council and report this as a violation of policy.

The Council representative will meet you for the verification visit at the prearranged location, at the time and date that was decided upon. She will ask you to present your photo ID for identification purposes.

The first order of business at the verification visit will be the Early Childhood Studies Review. This exam will assess your general knowledge and understanding of developmentally appropriate practices in programs for young children from birth through age five.

This exam will consist of sixty multiple-choice questions, with each question having four choices. The Council representative will give you a sealed test. You will not open it until she has explained all of the instructions and told you to begin.

Inside you'll find a Candidate Profile sheet, which you will complete with your personal information. The representative will go over two sample questions inside the booklet with you to make sure you understand how to decide on the correct answer and fill in the oval next to your choice. You will need a No. 2 pencil, so bring one or two along with you.

The Council representative will allow up to two hours for you to complete this exam, but it probably will not take that long. Those who finish early will be permitted to leave the room. You will not leave the premises, because you will be called one at a time for your oral interview after everyone has finished this sixty-question exam.

While you are working on the Early Childhood Studies Review, the Council representative will look over your documentation. She will use a checklist as she examines each item.

1. The Professional Resource File

   The Council representative will check to see whether these conditions are met:

   • Your autobiography is 200 to 300 words in length.

   • The file contains the six Competency Goal Statements.

   • It contains the seventeen resources.

   • You have included your original first-aid certificate.

   (The Council representative will return your Professional Resource File to you.)

2. Parent Opinion Questionnaires

   The Council representative will see whether these conditions are met:

   • They are each in a sealed envelope.

   • They are dated within six months of your application submission.

- At least 75 percent of the total number you distributed are enclosed.

(The Council representative is required to open all of the Parent Opinion Questionnaires. She will keep them.)

3. The CDA Assessment Observation Instrument

The Council representative will check to see whether these conditions are met:

- It is in a sealed envelope.

- It has been signed by your advisor.

- It has been dated within six months of your application submission.

- If you are an infant/toddler caregiver, the Supplemental Observation form is attached.

(The Council representative is required to open the Assessment Observation Instrument. She will keep it.)

4. The Competency Goal Statements

The Council representative will take a closer look at your Competency Goal Statements and will score them on the basis of specific criteria, making sure that these conditions are met:

- Each begins with the Competency Goal Statement *exactly* as written in the book.

- They are legible and can be easily read.

- Each statement is between 200 and 500 words long.

- They are written in *your own* words.

- The examples you have listed under each Functional Area are very specific and are *not* copied from the book.

- The examples reflect cultural and individual diversity.

- All of the Functional Areas under each Competency Goal have been covered.

The checklist and score sheet will be sent to the Council in Washington, DC, along with the copies of your autobiography and Competency Goal Statements, where they will be reviewed further.

When the Early Childhood Studies Review exam has been completed, the Council representative will begin the oral interview. If more than one candidate is at the verification visit, the representative will meet with each one individually. The other(s) will remain outside the room designated for the interviews and wait for their turns. Each candidate has as long as one and one-half hours for the interview, although it usually does not take nearly that long.

First, the Council representative will explain the procedures for the interview. You will discuss and give your own impressions concerning ten different scenarios that could happen in the type of early childhood program that matches your particular age-level endorsement and setting. So if you are a center-based infant/toddler care provider, the stories will be about children who are from birth through thirty-six months of age in a center-based setting. If you are a center-based preschool care provider, the stories will be about children who are three to five years old in a center-based setting. If you are a family child care provider, the stories will be about children from birth through five years old in a home setting. The ten stories will cover all of the Functional Areas, except Professionalism.

The Council representative will give you a copy of each situation, one at a time. They are on 9½-inch by 11-inch cards, each showing a black-and-white photo related to the story. The representative will also have a copy of the story and will read it aloud while you follow along on your copy. At the end of the story there will be a question asking what you think about the situation in the story. After the story and the question have been read, the representative will wait to listen to your comments.

When responding to the situation in the story, think about what is developmentally appropriate based on your experience and training, not what you would be expected to do at your present place of employment. Some of the situations may be examples of very good programs and practices, while others may not be. A situation may have some good points, but also some parts that are not very good. You will need to comment on both the good and the not-so-good parts of every situation.

The Council representative will be listening for you to touch on a few specific important aspects of the situation. Most of the time what the representative is expecting you to comment about will be rather obvious. From your training and experience, you should immediately recognize things in the story that seem appropriate, as well as those that do not. You will need to talk about why something seems appropriate to you or why it doesn't. You may also be asked what suggestions you have for doing something differently or better.

If you have made some comments about the story but have not given the information that the Council representative is expecting, she may ask you an additional question or two or refer you back to a specific part of the story in hopes you will give the appropriate response.

The Council representative is not allowed to tell you whether you have provided the correct information about the stories. She has to remain entirely objective; otherwise the accuracy of the interview will be compromised. Therefore, you should not ask her how you are doing or look for an accepting comment, nod, or smile after your responses. When all ten stories have been covered, the interview is over.

Remember, the oral interview is only one part of the credentialing process. The decision about whether a candidate will be awarded a CDA Credential is not based solely on this interview. All of the parts are considered, including the Early Childhood Studies Review, your Professional Resource File, the Competency Goal Statements, the Assessment Observation Instrument completed by your advisor, and the Parent Opinion Questionnaires.

Preparing for the Early Childhood Studies Review

7

THE EARLY CHILDHOOD STUDIES REVIEW will assess your general knowledge and understanding of developmentally appropriate practices in programs for young children who are ages birth through five. You will answer questions that cover this entire age range, regardless of whether you are in a center-based preschool, center-based infant/toddler, or family child care setting. The exam will consist of sixty multiple-choice questions, with each question having four answer choices.

Try the seventy-five practice questions, which start on the following page. Read each question and all of the answer choices carefully before choosing the best answer. After completion, use the answer key on page 147 to check your answers.

Practice Questions for the
Early Childhood Studies Review

1. The first-aid kit should be kept
   a. out of the reach of children.
   b. in an easily accessible location, clearly marked, and out of the reach of children.
   c. in a restroom.
   d. in a drawer far from where children will play.

2. Fire-exit information should be
   a. in written form.
   b. kept in a file labeled "Emergency Procedures."
   c. in both written and pictorial form, posted near the exits.
   d. in pictorial form.

3. Frequent hand washing is important because
   a. children need to keep hands clean.
   b. it keeps germs from spreading.
   c. it is a positive social skill.
   d. it is a law.

4. Choose the most healthy snack for young children:
   a. Saltine crackers and milk
   b. Orange juice and carrot sticks
   c. Oatmeal cookie and milk
   d. Apple slices, peanut butter, and milk

5. An open-ended question has
   a. one right answer.
   b. no right or wrong answer.
   c. two answers.
   d. a commonly repeated answer.

6. The amount of adult supervision that is needed depends on
   a. the number of children in the group.
   b. the activity.
   c. the developmental needs of children who are present.
   d. all of these.

7. Children should be provided with these items for washing their hands:

   a. Cold water, bar soap, and paper towels

   b. Hot water, liquid soap, and a cloth towel

   c. Warm water, liquid soap, and paper towels

   d. Water and paper towels

8. Children need their own spaces in the classroom for their coats and other belongings because

   a. it promotes their positive self-concept.

   b. it helps maintain good health.

   c. a and b.

   d. none of the above.

9. An example of a positive *nonverbal* communication is

   a. a smile.

   b. saying, "Good morning."

   c. ignoring a child's actions.

   d. moving away from a child.

10. At mealtime, a caregiver should

    a. insist that children finish all food on their plates.

    b. not offer any dessert until all their food is finished.

    c. only offer dessert to the children who remained quiet at the table while eating.

    d. none of the above.

11. When arranging a classroom, a teacher should

    a. keep the quiet and noisy activities together.

    b. put related activities near each other.

    c. provide a large, open area in the center of the room.

    d. arrange the furniture all along the walls.

12. The best example of an open-ended material would be

    a. an alphabet puzzle.

    b. playdough and cookie cutters.

    c. a coloring book and crayons.

    d. unit blocks.

13. Children's play materials should be kept
    a. in closed containers.
    b. on low, open shelves.
    c. on shelves out of their reach.
    d. in a storage cabinet to be taken out by the caregiver.

14. A developmentally appropriate schedule is one in which
    a. most of the day is spent in small-group activities.
    b. most of the day is spent in guided free play.
    c. children spend most of their time sitting at tables.
    d. children spend most of the day outside on the playground.

15. A developmentally appropriate group time
    a. lasts only a short time.
    b. gets the children actively involved.
    c. permits children to leave, if they wish.
    d. all of the above.

16. Why do you give children a warning before activities are about to change?
    a. It gives them time to clean up their toys.
    b. It provides them time to finish an activity.
    c. It helps quickly get their attention.
    d. It is a signal to come to the next activity right away.

17. A good early childhood practice is
    a. having the children line up to use the restroom.
    b. having the children sit outside the restroom to wait for their turn.
    c. having the children all do an art activity together.
    d. asking the children to pretend to be butterflies as they walk to the playground.

18. An activity that develops small-motor skills would be
    a. swinging.
    b. beanbag throwing.
    c. bead stringing.
    d. jumping.

19. An activity that develops small-motor skills would be

    a. manipulating playdough.

    b. walking on a balance beam.

    c. throwing a ball.

    d. riding a tricycle.

20. When you provide an activity that lets children use their senses of smell, sight, hearing, touch, and taste, it promotes

    a. physical development.

    b. social development.

    c. cognitive development.

    d. communication development.

21. Two boys want the same truck to haul blocks across the room. One boy goes to the housekeeping area and gets a basket. This is

    a. an open-ended question.

    b. an example of problem solving.

    c. a small-motor exercise.

    d. guidance.

22. When talking with a child, the caregiver should

    a. speak loudly.

    b. get down to the child's eye level.

    c. whisper softly to the child.

    d. stand and talk with the child.

23. Caregivers should

    a. control the conversations that children have with them.

    b. be good listeners.

    c. ask a lot of open-ended questions.

    d. both b and c.

24. Children's artwork should be

    a. put on bulletin boards in the hallways.

    b. placed high on walls so other children cannot touch them.

    c. displayed at the children's eye level.

    d. put immediately into the children's cubbies to be taken home.

25. A creative art project is

   a. marble painting on turkey shapes.

   b. painting at the easel on pumpkin-shaped paper with orange and black paint.

   c. painting with orange and black paint on white paper.

   d. sponge painting on a white ghost shape.

26. A creative activity is

   a. cooking using a recipe.

   b. stringing beads.

   c. using playdough.

   d. assembling a twenty-piece puzzle.

27. Which activity is creative?

   a. Using a CD that tells children how to move

   b. Dancing to an instrumental CD with scarves

   c. Using musical instruments with a CD that tells children when to play them

   d. Singing "Where is Thumbkin?"

28. CDA stands for

   a. Child's Dental Assistant.

   b. Child Development Associate.

   c. Child Development Association.

   d. Child Development Administration.

29. A CDA is

   a. a licensing agency for early childhood professionals.

   b. the only nationally recognized early childhood credential.

   c. an association for early childhood administrators.

   d. a program offered by certain states.

30. Guidance/discipline and punishment are

   a. different ways of saying the same thing.

   b. different approaches to helping children become competent.

   c. neither of the above.

   d. both a and b.

31. A good technique for dealing with favorite toys is to

    a. provide duplicates of them.

    b. put them away when children squabble over them.

    c. provide them as rewards for good behavior.

    d. none of the above.

32. A large circle time with all the children involved is

    a. necessary for good overall development.

    b. done for very brief periods of time.

    c. not a good idea for children under age three.

    d. both b and c.

33. A positive circle experience includes

    a. scheduling and planning beforehand.

    b. interesting and active activities.

    c. anticipating problems beforehand.

    d. all of the above.

34. Appropriate choices for young children include this statement:

    a. "Whatever you would like to do today!"

    b. "You may have ice cream or oranges for snack today."

    c. "You may choose from the art area, the housekeeping area, or the puzzle table."

    d. None of the above.

35. Good practice provides children the opportunity to "live with diversity." Which of the following statements best represents that statement?

    a. There are children of mixed heritages in the classroom.

    b. Pictures, learning materials, and posters depict children and families of diverse backgrounds, ages, abilities, and sexes including, but not limited to, materials that portray the dominant culture of the room.

    c. The classroom celebrates Black History Month.

    d. Teachers offer children a piñata and make tacos on Cinco de Mayo.

36. Situations that reflect bias include
    a. Thanksgiving stories that depict Indians with war paint and headdresses.
    b. Halloween stories with pictures where everything black is portrayed as scary.
    c. block activities that serve to exclude girls and housekeeping activities that are offered first to girls.
    d. all of the above.

37. Appropriate guidance techniques would include
    a. planning to avoid problems with the use of space, placement and number of toys, and careful supervision.
    b. interacting with children in positive ways.
    c. redirecting inappropriate behavior.
    d. all of the above.

38. Fine-motor skills refer to skills that
    a. children need to move to the next developmental level.
    b. require children to work with their hands and fingers.
    c. enable children to walk on a balance beam or on a straight line.
    d. none of the above.

39. Gross-motor skills refer to skills that
    a. require children to make large movements with their bodies.
    b. require children to participate in messy activities.
    c. require children to use scissors or eyedroppers.
    d. none of the above.

40. Children learn best when they
    a. actively participate.
    b. follow directions carefully.
    c. both a and b.
    d. none of the above.

41. Coloring books, ABC worksheets, and offering sample artwork are
    a. activities that strengthen skills.
    b. developmentally appropriate.
    c. not developmentally appropriate.
    d. activities that should be offered every day.

42. Playing double Dutch with a jump rope, games with rules, and riding a two-wheeled bicycle

    a. would be frustrating for most preschoolers.

    b. should be offered on a preschool playground.

    c. are activities for gifted children.

    d. none of the above.

43. Experience charts, labeling items in the room, and making lots of books available are all examples of

    a. practices that support emergent literacy.

    b. practices children will encounter once they begin elementary school.

    c. practices that should be provided only to older preschoolers.

    d. none of the above.

44. A writing center for preschoolers should include

    a. a variety of alphabet worksheets with letters to trace.

    b. pencils, paper, markers, envelopes, an old typewriter, and pieces of old mail.

    c. both a and b.

    d. none of the above.

45. Scribbling is

    a. something that should be discouraged.

    b. an indication of a developmental delay in preschool children.

    c. an early stage in the development of children's art and writing skills.

    d. none of the above.

46. Choose the most appropriate themes from the following list:

    a. Pets, water, trucks, friends

    b. Famous Americans, first Thanksgiving, Easter

    c. Both of the above

    d. None of the above

47. To extend a "teachable moment,"

    a. observe what is happening.

    b. describe what is happening and ask open-ended questions.

    c. let children come up with ideas about what they would like to do.

    d. all of the above.

48. Children's artwork should

    a. be recognizable so their parents can appreciate it.

    b. emphasize the process rather than the product.

    c. both of the above.

    d. none of the above.

49. The following materials and activities are appropriate ways to help preschoolers prepare for reading:

    a. Flash cards, workbooks, worksheets, and phonics lessons

    b. Magnetic letters, a well-stocked book corner, and reading to them every day

    c. Learning "The Alphabet Song"

    d. None of the above

50. A good way to get a new child and his or her family off to a positive start is to

    a. invite them to visit before the first day.

    b. provide the family with written information about the program and answer questions they might have.

    c. none of the above.

    d. both of the above.

51. Positive ways to involve parents in the program include

    a. wiping tables.

    b. reading stories.

    c. cleaning up the bathroom.

    d. all of the above.

52. An important part of a quality early childhood program is for caregivers to communicate with parents. Some examples would be

    a. parent (or guardian) conferences.

    b. parent (or guardian) meetings.

    c. conversations at arrival and departure times.

    d. all of the above.

53. Parent/teacher conflicts happen. A positive way to resolve them is to

    a. practice active listening.

    b. suggest the parents look over their copy of your program's parent handbook, referring to sections that may clear up misunderstandings and address the problem.

c. both of the above.

d. none of the above.

54. When the caregiver needs a substitute, the most important thing to do is

a. introduce the substitute and the children to each other.

b. have written plans for the substitute to follow.

c. provide the substitute with a listing of program expectations.

d. all of the above.

55. Professional relationships with other staff include

a. attending professional development events together, such as conferences and workshops.

b. spending time planning cooperatively to meet the needs of the children.

c. treating each other with respect.

d. all of the above.

56. Community resource information for the parents should be available

a. from the caregiver.

b. from the director.

c. both of the above.

d. none of the above.

57. Information that is gathered about the children should be

a. shared with specialists when the parents or guardians refuse to seek help for their child.

b. shared with parents.

c. discussed only among the caregivers who know the children.

d. all of the above.

58. A milestone of development is

a. a definite point in a child's life.

b. a part of motor development.

c. a functional skill or task that most children can do at a certain age range.

d. none of the above.

59. The following are characteristics of typical three- through five-year-old ranges of development:

   a. Children match letters with those in their name.

   b. Children create make-believe stories.

   c. Children can recognize a number of different colors.

   d. All of the above.

60. Teachers can support characteristic development of three-through five-year-old children by

   a. writing down the children's stories.

   b. requiring that they sit quietly and complete coloring pages or worksheets.

   c. both of the above.

   d. none of the above.

61. Preschoolers will use shocking language. An appropriate response would be

   a. putting the child in time-out, isolating him or her from the rest of the children.

   b. telling the child that such language is not appropriate.

   c. giving the child a lot of attention each time he or she uses such language.

   d. all of the above.

62. Children who are between eighteen months and two years old can typically

   a. scribble with markers.

   b. write their names.

   c. draw pictures that are recognizable.

   d. none of the above.

63. The typical toddler

   a. understands more words than he or she can say.

   b. is possessive about his or her belongings.

   c. sits and listens to short stories.

   d. all of the above.

64. A caregiver can encourage a toddler's development by

   a. trying to toilet train as soon as possible.

   b. engaging the child in conversations and repeating some of what he or she says so the child can hear the words.

c. waiting to provide eating utensils until the child is at least three years old.

d. none of the above.

65. Behaviors of the typical three- to four-year-old child include
   a. playing alongside other children in small groups.
   b. increasing small-muscle control.
   c. not being able to recognize racial differences.
   d. both a and b.

66. Children who are three through four years old should be able to
   a. wait patiently in line.
   b. make a choice from two or three that are given.
   c. follow rules without being supervised.
   d. understand the consequences of their own behavior.

67. Teachers can provide support to the three- to four-year-old child by
   a. providing verbal reprimands for toileting accidents.
   b. providing worksheets to reinforce skills.
   c. using ABC flash cards.
   d. using letters and numbers as they come up in real situations.

68. The purpose of observing children is to
   a. compare the growth and development among children in the group.
   b. identify patterns of their growth and development.
   c. provide the teachers with information so they can plan appropriate activities for the children.
   d. both b and c.

69. Some types of observation tools are
   a. anecdotal records.
   b. running records and child interviews.
   c. developmental checklists.
   d. all of the above.

70. When you are preparing an environment for children, what should always be considered first?
   a. State licensing regulations
   b. Center policy

c. Safety of the child

d. CDA standards

71. Classroom rules and rules for outdoor safety should be

a. few in number.

b. worded in simple terms, using pictures.

c. written in positive terms, saying what the children *should* be doing.

d. all of the above.

72. Child abuse and neglect reporting is the responsibility of

a. the teacher.

b. the person who observed the incident.

c. the director.

d. the social service or regulatory agency.

73. Universal Procedures refers to

a. procedures that are taught in universal preschool programs.

b. procedures for containing, disposing, and cleaning up body fluids.

c. a checklist used by state licensing inspectors.

d. all of the above.

74. An appropriate mealtime would include

a. a well-balanced meal that meets licensing regulations.

b. pleasant conversation at the table.

c. encouragement to eat.

d. all of the above.

75. A balanced schedule would include

a. a good deal of teacher-directed activities.

b. outdoor time only when all of the children have brought appropriate clothing.

c. long periods of quiet activities.

d. none of the above.

Answer Key to Practice Questions
for the Early Childhood Studies Review

1. b	21. b	41. c	61. b
2. c	22. b	42. a	62. a
3. b	23. d	43. a	63. d
4. d	24. c	44. b	64. b
5. b	25. c	45. c	65. d
6. d	26. c	46. a	66. b
7. c	27. b	47. d	67. d
8. b	28. b	48. b	68. d
9. a	29. b	49. b	69. d
10. d	30. b	50. d	70. c
11. b	31. a	51. b	71. d
12. d	32. d	52. d	72. b
13. b	33. d	53. c	73. b
14. b	34. c	54. d	74. d
15. d	35. b	55. d	75. d
16. b	36. d	56. c	
17. d	37. d	57. b	
18. c	38. b	58. c	
19. a	39. a	59. d	
20. c	40. a	60. a	

Preparing for the Oral Interview

8

THE ORAL INTERVIEW WILL ASSESS your knowledge and expertise as you respond to several early childhood scenarios. These scenarios will relate to your specific age-level endorsement and setting.

To prepare for the oral interview, look over the following four stories that correspond to your specific setting and the age level of the children with whom you work. As you read each story, think about what immediately strikes you as developmentally appropriate and an example of good practices. Then change your perspective. Using your knowledge and experience from similar situations, analyze the story for evidence of practices that you feel are inappropriate or could be handled differently. Jot down your ideas on a piece of paper.

When you have finished working through all four stories, look at the answer suggestions and see whether you touched on most or all of their key points. If you missed a few points, go back and reread the story so you understand what you may have overlooked.

Center-Based Preschool Oral Interview Practice Scenarios

1. Melissa likes using the classroom computer. She especially likes the alphabet game and spends every morning playing it. Mrs. Harris is becoming concerned that Melissa is not taking part in the other activities in the room and is not socializing with the other children very

much. Mrs. Harris decides to ask Melissa's friend Nathan to join Melissa at the computer. This way Melissa will have the chance to work and socialize with someone and still be able to participate in the activity of her choice. Comment on this situation.

2. Marta and Will are co-teachers for a group of eleven four-year-olds. They take turns supervising when the children go outside on the playground. One of them will stand near the play equipment. The other will take a short break on a bench nearby, while keeping an eye on the situation. If the supervising teacher needs assistance, the other teacher will come over right away to help. Comment on this situation.

3. Mrs. Nevins teaches a group of three-year-olds. Many of the parents have expressed concern that the children have been spending too much time playing and are not being provided with enough academics in preparation for school. So Mrs. Nevins now has the children sit at tables every morning to complete a worksheet about letters or numbers. The children are not permitted to leave the table to play until they finish the activity. Yesterday, one of the children began to cry because he didn't want to work at the table any longer. Mrs. Nevins was able to encourage him to keep working and to eventually finish most of the page. Comment on this situation.

4. Many of the children in Mrs. Allen's preschool room have colds this week and it seems she is always wiping noses in between her other tasks with the children. After a nose is wiped, Mrs. Allen has the child put his own tissue in the wastebasket before returning to play. That way she does not have to continually wash her hands. Comment on this situation.

Answer suggestions for the center-based preschool oral interview practice scenarios

1. Mrs. Harris knows the computer doesn't have to be a solitary activity and children can work together on computer programs. Mrs. Harris has arranged for someone who has similar interests and computer abilities to join Melissa at the computer. This way Melissa will have the opportunity to socialize and still be able to

participate in the activity she chooses. Mrs. Harris may also want to encourage Melissa to try other activities in the room by using a simple timer at the computer. She can make the time policy with the entire group during circle time, so everyone knows how much time they will have at the computer before moving to another activity. By Mrs. Harris making it a classroom policy, rather than just a special one for Melissa, Melissa may accept it more readily.

2. Whether indoors or outdoors, both caregivers must share equally in playing with and supervising the young children in their group. Outdoor playtime is not an opportunity for care providers to take a break. Four-year-olds are active risk takers and one caregiver would not be able to adequately supervise eleven of them on play equipment. If something happened, the one supervising teacher might not even see it, making this a major liability issue.

3. Mrs. Nevins evidently knew the value that play has in the overall development of young children because it was a predominant part of the daily schedule. The children's parents, however, may not have understood this when they expressed their desire for a more academic curriculum. Rather than compromising her philosophy of appropriate practice, Mrs. Nevins should explain to the parents how children learn many skills through their play. She might invite them into the classroom to observe and then point out what the children are learning as they play in the different areas of the room.

4. The large number of children with colds was probably caused by poor hygiene practices in this classroom. Mrs. Allen should have a lined and covered wastebasket available to keep the germs contained. Having the children dispose of their own tissues does not keep the germs off Mrs. Allen's hands after she helps them blow their noses. Nowhere in this scenario does anyone wash hands, neither the children nor their caregiver. Frequent hand washing with warm water, liquid soap, and paper towels is one of the most effective ways to prevent the spread of germs and, unless this procedure is practiced, the children will continue to pass their colds to one another, and perhaps to Mrs. Allen as well.

Center-Based Infant/Toddler Oral Interview Practice Scenarios

1. Adam provides the infants with lots of tummy time on a safe area of the floor. The infants are encouraged to look at interesting and colorful objects and to move and reach for them. Adam also changes the infants' positions often so they can enjoy different areas and surfaces. Comment on this situation.

2. When the toddlers begin to get restless and lose interest in the activity she has put out on the table, Rhonda plays a DVD they enjoy. Some of the children will watch for quite a while and others fall asleep. The ones who won't sit still are given a cookie and juice to settle down. Comment on this situation. What are your ideas for improving this situation?

3. Miss Kay provides a good variety of age-appropriate toys for the infants in her group. Although she has duplicates of many of them, very often two children will still want the same toy. When this happens, Miss Kay will take the toy away and put it in the storage cabinet. How else could Miss Kay handle this situation?

4. Sherita and her assistant have five infants in their room. They usually hold the infants for feedings and play with them while they are awake. Sherita will often let the infants stay in their cribs after awakening from a nap for up to a half hour so she can provide one-on-one time with the others. Comment on this situation.

Answer suggestions for the center-based infant/toddler oral interview practice scenarios

1. Adam seems to understand how to promote the physical and cognitive development of infants. By having time on their tummies, the infants are given the opportunity to lift their heads and upper bodies, strengthening their necks, arms, shoulders, and torsos. Adam encourages them to reach and move, using a variety of colorful toys. Adam does not leave the infants in the same position or location for extended periods of time. New perspectives and things to explore stimulate their overall development.

2. DVDs and videos should not be used on a regular basis. Children probably already spend too much time in front of a TV screen at home and don't need any additional hours in child care. Perhaps Rhonda needs to re-evaluate the activities that she plans to find out why the children are losing interest. Rhonda may be expecting the children to participate in the activities for long periods of time, which would not be realistic for this age group. Rhonda should not be giving the children cookies and juice to settle them down. Using food to control behavior is inappropriate and gives children the wrong message about why food is eaten. It appears this is being done outside of the regular snacktime, which will interfere with the children's appetite for healthier foods later.

3. Providing duplicates of popular toys is a good way to avoid many, but not all, squabbles over the same one. Very young children may not realize there is more than one of the toy they are focused on. Instead of taking the toy away from both children, Miss Kay can provide the duplicate to one of them, which may eliminate their frustration. If this doesn't work, Miss Kay can redirect one or both children to a different activity or toys for the time being.

4. It is good that these two caregivers hold the infants for feedings and spend time playing with them; however, the practice of leaving them in their cribs after they awaken from their naps is not appropriate. Infants are forming attachments with their caregivers. To nurture this attachment, the caregivers should be responsive to their needs. Picking them up from their cribs when they are awake helps build their sense of trust. Cribs should be used only for sleeping, not as playpens or parking spots when the caregivers are doing other things. While awake, infants should spend most of their day on a safe, supervised area of the floor, free to move around, with stimulating toys and activities that are suited to their developmental levels. Also, caregivers should be checking the children's diapers when they wake from their naps, not postponing this task until it is more convenient.

Family Child Care Oral Interview Practice Scenarios

1. Mrs. Wilson provides art for the four-year-olds every day. She gives each of them a page from her thick coloring book and the children are asked to choose two colors from the crayon box. After they finish coloring, Mrs. Wilson prints their names across the top of the pages and hangs them on the refrigerator until they go home. Mrs. Wilson lets the parents and guardians know whether their child has done a good job staying inside the lines or whether they need to work with their child on this skill at home. Comment on this situation.

2. Mary Kay wants to find out why Robert has been pushing his friends all morning. She goes over to him and kneels down to his level, putting her hand on his shoulder. She asks him to tell her about what has been happening. She maintains eye contact and repeats back what he says to her, so he knows she's really listening and understands. She then asks him for some ideas for solving the problem and offers to help him carry them out. Comment on this situation.

3. Barbara wanted to provide separate spaces for each of the children to keep their belongings but there wasn't enough room in her home for cubbies. So Barbara's husband installed wooden pegs along the hallway and Barbara sewed each child a large, drawstring bag for belongings. She then made labels with their printed names and hung them above the pegs. Comment on this situation.

4. Ian's mother brings nine-month-old Ian in his car seat every morning. He always seems content to stay in his car seat as long as he has something interesting to hold or a bottle of milk. Since Ann also cares for three preschoolers, she finds it easier to leave him in the car seat, as long as he is happy there. Otherwise she has to worry about him getting stepped on by the older children or getting into things. How else could Ann handle this situation?

Answer suggestions for the family child care oral interview practice scenarios

1. While it is good that Mrs. Wilson sees the value in providing the children with art activities on a regular basis, providing them with coloring pages and crayons

is not a good choice. Young children need opportunities for creative expression with opportunities to enjoy the *process* of art, rather than focusing on a finished product. A coloring page is a *closed-ended* activity, with the child being given predrawn images to be filled in with color. This does not allow much creativity. Mrs. Wilson limited the possibility for the children's creativity by allowing the children to use only two different colors. Instead, Mrs. Wilson could provide the children with *open-ended* art activities, such as painting, molding with clay or playdough, or drawing on large sheets of plain paper with a large assortment of markers or crayons. Coloring inside the lines on a coloring sheet is not an important skill for preschoolers. It is not something Mrs. Wilson should be assessing, nor something parents and guardians should feel the need to work on at home with their children. Instead, she could point out the kinds of art their children enjoy and offer suggestions for other creative activities they could participate in together.

2. Mary Kay has been observing Robert and she has seen new behaviors that are not typical for him. Instead of merely redirecting and providing consequences for these behaviors, she has decided to try to find out what may be causing them, so a solution can be found. Mary Kay knows that if she wants Robert to talk with her, she has to get down to his level and show a sincere interest in what he has to say. She asks him questions and then waits for him to respond. She uses *active listening,* repeating what he has said back to him, which lets Robert know she is really listening to him and helps Mary Kay find out whether she understands what he wants to say. Then instead of telling him what she wants him to do, Mary Kay asks Robert to come up with some of his own ideas for solving the problem and she offers her support in carrying them out.

3. Barbara came up with a feasible solution to separate storage for the children in the limited space she has. However, she has made all the bags from the same fabric, which may cause some confusion about whose bag is whose. Using different fabrics or making each different in some other way might help this work better. Barbara might also want to consider storage that is not fabric, since it may harbor germs if not washed frequently. Instead, she might use plastic crates or some shelving under the row of

hooks for additional space. The name tags Barbara made for each child are a good idea, but they may be too high on the wall for the children to see easily.

4. It is good that Ann provides Ian with interesting toys to discover. However, no child should be left in a car seat or other device for any length of time. Ian should be provided with safe areas on the floor to move around and develop his large-motor skills and coordination. Children who are Ian's age are typically preparing to walk and, if given the chance, Ian would probably learn to pull himself up and begin to cruise around the furniture. Keeping him in a car seat may impede his normal development. Although it may be more convenient for Ann to give Ian a bottle, a child who is nine months old is usually able to drink from a cup. She should give him the opportunity to do so. Also, providing Ian with a bottle of milk to keep him pacified gives him the wrong message about the reasons for eating. If Ann is concerned for Ian's safety when he is out of the car seat, she could prepare a place in the room for him to play away from the general traffic areas used by the preschoolers and the materials she does not want him to touch. If Ann has properly childproofed the areas of her home where she operates her family child care program, there shouldn't be too much for Ian to get into, besides the preschoolers' materials, and she can make sure those items are kept away from his reach.

Reflecting on Your Responses

You probably touched on several or perhaps all of the main points of these scenarios in your reflections. Perhaps you have contact with others who are also working on or have already earned the CDA Credential. It would be valuable to discuss these scenarios in a small group for better understanding.

As mentioned earlier, your CDA advisor can often be a valuable resource as you go through the CDA process. If you work in a child care center, your director can also be a source of support. The following chapter is devoted to center directors and how they can help ensure the success of their teachers who are working on a CDA Credential. It would be a good idea to encourage your director to read it so you might benefit from the added support only a director can provide.

A Word to Center-Based Program Directors: Supporting Your CDA Candidates

9

IF YOU ARE A CENTER DIRECTOR, you are faced with making sure your staff members acquire the training and qualifications they need to meet licensing requirements and to provide the best possible care for the children in your program. In light of recent research indicating the importance of the first five years of life for children's optimal development, the Child Development Associate (CDA) Credential has become the basic, required qualification for leading child care providers in most states. The Council for Professional Recognition is the agency headquartered in Washington, DC, that awards the CDA Credential. You can find a state-by-state listing of such requirements on the Council's website at www.cdacouncil.org. Click on "The Resource Center" and then "National Training Directory."

Quality child care depends on qualified, trained staff, period. Whether you have requested your teachers get the CDA Credential or they have taken the honorable initiative to improve themselves through this process, the bottom line is the same: increased quality for your center. To be successful in earning the CDA Credential, your teachers will need not only to work hard to prepare themselves for the process but also an appropriate setting in which they can be observed by their CDA advisors.

As the director of the center, you play a very important role. You can be a source of support and help for your CDA candidate. In a sense, when a teacher is working toward a credential, the entire program is too. If you have asked that your teachers get the CDA Credential, your responsibility doesn't end there. They will not be going through this process as separate entities but will be using your center as the setting for their assessment observation. If the setting does not meet the standards required by the Council, your teachers will have a difficult time passing the formal assessment observation.

Working toward a CDA Credential requires a good deal of effort on a teacher's part, including 120 clock hours of formal early childhood training, assembling a comprehensive Professional Resource File, and writing six Competency Goal Statements, each of which is about 500 words in length. Can you imagine the disappointment and frustration a teacher would experience if she had come this far, completed all the required training and documentation, and then realized the center where the assessment observation was to take place wouldn't work…or worse yet, the director was not willing to do what it took to *make* it work?

Answers to Questions That Center Directors Frequently Ask

The following are some common questions asked by center directors, along with answers that may help you better understand the task ahead for your candidate.

Who will come to my center?

The person who will come to your center will be the candidate's CDA advisor. The advisor is acting as a representative of the Council for Professional Recognition in Washington, DC. The advisor's job is to assess the candidate's work with young children in a qualified early childhood setting and to report back to the Council.

The advisor is usually a qualified early childhood professional from the local area who has agreed to assume this task. Often, the person is a faculty member from the institution where the candidate received her CDA training hours, an experienced early care and education provider from another program, or someone on the Council's list of advisors.

The advisor will make one or two observation visits, totaling three to four hours. The advisor can give you valuable information and suggestions related to your program. Be sure to get to know and spend some time with the advisor.

What will the advisor be looking for at my center?

For your teacher to demonstrate her knowledge and expertise in working with young children, she will need a classroom with appropriate equipment, materials, health and safety features, and operating procedures.

If one of your teachers is working on a CDA Credential, she probably has sent for and received a CDA application packet. In the packet are two copies of the *CDA Assessment System and Competency Standards* book. They will either be yellow for an infant/toddler setting or green for a preschool setting. Ask to borrow one of the books so you can familiarize yourself with the Council's criteria for an appropriate setting.

If one of these books is not available, you can order one yourself from the Council. If your program serves infants, toddlers, and preschoolers, you'll probably want to order both books. The cost of each book is about $8, but check with the Council because this price is subject to change.

What if something isn't the way it should be?

If your teacher or the CDA advisor has indicated a problem area in your teacher's classroom, do your best to remedy the situation. Usually it is something minor and easily fixed. If you need clarification on exactly what is required, be sure to ask the advisor.

I understand my teacher will be observed by a CDA advisor. I have also been told that she will participate in a verification visit conducted by a representative of the CDA Council. If the Council representative decides to conduct the verification visit at my center, will she be evaluating the classroom too?

No. The only person who will conduct an observation at your center will be the candidate's advisor.

If this is a licensed center, I have nothing to worry about, right?

Wrong! State licensing is a minimum operating standard for child care facilities. It does little to address developmentally appropriate practices and what is considered "quality" in an early childhood program. Read the information found in the *CDA Assessment System and Competency Standards* books and conduct the self-study provided on page 161 to familiarize yourself with the standards to which a CDA candidate will be held. By understanding exactly what the Council representative will be looking for during the assessment observation, you can better support your teacher candidate.

Do the families in my program play any part in this process?

Yes. The parents' or guardians' opinions of a candidate's work with their children are a very important part of assessing competency. For this reason, the candidate will distribute Parent Opinion Questionnaires provided by the Council to the parents or guardians of the children she teaches. Ask to see one of the blank questionnaires before they are distributed by the candidate. These questionnaires will be placed in sealed envelopes by the parents or guardians and given by the candidate to the Council representative. The candidate needs to have about 75 percent of these questionnaires returned to her, so it might be helpful to encourage the parents to return them in a timely fashion.

Some of my other teachers who are not working on the CDA Credential feel a little nervous and threatened by my teacher who is. Is this normal and how should I handle it?

This happens, especially with teachers who have been at the center for many years. They may feel threatened by a coworker who is working to gain additional child care training and who is learning new and better ways of working with young children. These teachers may be afraid they will have to make abrupt changes in their usual ways of doing things or may even fear losing their jobs to other teachers who are better trained. Some teachers don't care to be told to do things differently than they have been doing for many years, especially if it is by a younger teacher with new ideas. At other times, staff members may be unclear or have false information about what a CDA Credential is and what is required to earn one.

It is in the center's best interest to put these misunderstandings and fears to rest. At a staff meeting, explain the CDA process or have someone come in to speak to the staff and hand out informational materials. Explain your center's policy of teamwork and support, and encourage the rest of the staff to consider becoming a CDA, as well.

Above all, do *not* allow other staff members to treat your CDA candidate unfairly or with disrespect. Let the other teachers know that you value what this teacher is doing and she has your full support, and they should do likewise.

Should a center director consider becoming a CDA?

Absolutely! Unless you have an associate's or a bachelor's degree in early childhood education, becoming a CDA would be a crucial part of any director's credentials and may even be required in your state. In any event, what an excellent example you would set for every member of your staff!

I'm ready to help my teachers. Where do I begin?

You can begin by doing a self-study of your program using the *CDA Assessment System and Competency Standards* book. Take notes on particular areas that do *not* meet the Council's Competency Standards. It is in your best interest to correct those items, because they will affect your teacher's ability to get a CDA Credential in your center. Also, since the Competency Standards reflect developmentally appropriate practices and are modeled closely after the standards of the National Association for the Education of Young Children (NAEYC), you will enhance the quality of your program as a whole. If you plan to seek NAEYC accreditation in the future, complying with the Competency Standards is definitely a step in the right direction!

If you have the aforementioned CDA books, begin your self-study at Functional Area 1: Safe as outlined on pages 39–41 in the yellow book and pages 39–41 in the green book. Here are some important items to be aware of:

- The facility should be generally safe and free from hazards. The furniture should be in good repair with no broken toys or other materials.
- Electrical cords should not be within the children's reach. For example, when a cassette player is plugged in, is the cord exposed?
- When an outlet is not being used, it should have plastic safety caps inserted.
- A first-aid kit with basic supplies should be in every classroom. If the kit is inside a cabinet, the cabinet door should be labeled to indicate where the kit is located.
- Emergency procedures (escape route, choking, Universal Procedures, basic first aid, CPR, etc.) should be posted in the room.
- A listing or file of emergency contact numbers for the children should be located in the room for easy access.
- A listing should be available of persons authorized to pick up the children from your center.
- Area rugs should be secured to the floor.

- The outdoor playground should be safe. An adequate amount of some type of cushioning material needs to be in place under climbers, slides, and swings. Rusted or otherwise damaged equipment needs to be removed.

- Miniblind cords should be wound up and out of reach.

Functional Area 2: Healthy is covered on pages 42–45 in the yellow book and pages 42–44 in the green book. Some important items to be aware of include the following:

- Floors and carpeting should be clean.

- Covers on cots and crib sheets need to be washed at least weekly. They need to be clean at all times.

- Cots should be sanitized often and children's bedding materials kept separate.

- Toys and surfaces should be washed/sanitized daily.

- Health and immunization records should be kept up to date for each child.

- The facility should smell clean. There are no unpleasant odors.

- Covered, plastic-lined trash cans should be available in each room.

- Restrooms should be clean. Warm water, liquid soap, and paper towels should be available for the children to use.

- The focus of snacks and meals should be good nutrition. No processed foods or junk foods should be offered.

- Milk, water, or 100 percent fruit juices should be the only acceptable beverage choices.

Functional Area 3: Learning Environment is covered on pages 46–49 in the yellow book and pages 45–47 in the green book. Here are some important items to be aware of:

- Books, toys, and other materials should be appropriate to the developmental level(s) of the children.

- Books and materials should reflect cultural diversity and anti-bias (multicultural dolls, posters showing children of various ethnic and racial groups, no sexist or stereotypical items).

- Children's toys and materials should be stored on low, open shelves in easily accessible containers/bins that encourage independent use and cleanup.

- A step stool should be provided at the sink, if necessary, so children can wash hands by themselves.

- Child-sized furniture (tables and chairs) should be available.

- An ample variety of toys and materials, as well as duplicates of many toys, should be available.

- The room should be set up in "centers" so the children, including toddlers, can have opportunities to make choices during free play. These activity centers may include the following:
  - Dramatic play
  - Blocks
  - Art
  - Water table
  - Sand table
  - Book corner
  - Manipulatives
  - Easel

- Children should not all be doing the same activity at the same time. For example, the whole group of toddlers should not sit down at a table for art. Art and other activities should be offered as choices during free play.

- Circle time for young children should be very short and should consist of songs, fingerplays, short stories, movement activities, and the like. There should be no flash cards or drills.

Functional Area 4: Physical is covered on pages 50–52 in the yellow book and pages 48–50 in the green book. Here are some items to note:

- Infants should be given ample "tummy time" on a clean floor surface so they can explore and strengthen their upper bodies.

- Infants should spend only *short* periods of time in infant seats, bouncers, or swings.

- Children should have a daily opportunity for large-motor activities, indoors and outdoors.

- There should be a wide variety of interesting, appropriate, and safe toys for infants and toddlers.

Functional Area 5: Cognitive is covered on pages 53–56 in the yellow book and pages 51–53 in the green book. Here are some items to note:

- Large blocks of guided free-play time should be offered.

- Lots of interaction should occur between the children and caregivers. Caregivers should play with the children at every opportunity.

- Emphasis should be on children learning through play, with hands-on experiences.

- Activities are available that provide opportunities for problem solving.

Functional Area 6: Communication is covered on pages 57–60 in the yellow book and pages 54–57 in the green book. Here are some items to note:

- There should be a constant flow of communication with the children, one on one, at their eye level.

- Caregivers should be good language models for the children.

- An ample number of quality children's books should be available.

Functional Area 7: Creative is covered on pages 61–63 in the yellow book and pages 58–60 in the green book. Here are some items to note:

- Provide unstructured play materials, such as blocks, paint, playdough, and musical instruments.

- Provide "messy" activities for children, such as fingerpainting, water and sand play, and watercolor markers.

- Allow toddlers to participate in creative art activities and with many of the same unstructured play materials as preschoolers on a limited basis.

- Art activities should emphasize the process rather than a finished product of some kind.

Functional Area 8: Self is covered on pages 64–67 in the yellow book and pages 61–63 in the green book. Here are some items to note:

- Allow children to make choices in their activities.

- Provide one-on-one attention whenever possible.

- Respond quickly to an infant's distress.

- Hold and cuddle infants as much as possible.

- Give hugs and affection to toddlers and preschoolers.

- Display photos of the children and their families at the children's eye level in the room.

Functional Area 9: Social is covered on pages 68–70 in the yellow book and pages 64–65 in the green book. Here are some items to note:

- Provide duplicates of popular toys.

- Provide consistent caregivers for infants and young children to promote attachment and bonding.

- Show positive social role-modeling through care providers treating each other with respect.

Functional Area 10: Guidance is covered on pages 71–74 in the yellow book and pages 66–68 in the green book. Here are some items to note:

- Use *positive* guidance methods, such as redirection, listening, and reinforcement.

- Have realistic expectations of young children's interests, attention spans, physical needs, and social abilities.

Functional Area 11: Families is covered on pages 75–78 in the yellow book and pages 69–72 in the green book. Some items to note include the following:

- Display a parent bulletin board with news of upcoming events, parenting tips, and child development information in every room.

- Communicate with families in several ways, including newsletters and periodic conferences with the teachers.

- Encourage families to visit the center and participate in activities.

Functional Area 12: Program Management is covered on pages 79–81 in the yellow book and pages 73–75 in the green book. Here are some items to note:

- Maintain up-to-date health and immunization records on all children attending the center.

- Provide regularly scheduled staff meetings and in-service training opportunities.

- Provide proper training for staff and encourage professional development.

Functional Area 13: Professionalism is covered on pages 82–84 in the yellow book and pages 76–78 in the green book. Here are some items to note:

- The staff in the center should enjoy working with young children.

- Staff members should be continually seeking to improve themselves by attending training courses and conferences.

- Staff members should join professional organizations, such as NAEYC.
- Staff members should be committed to a policy of confidentiality with the families in the program.

Tips and suggestions from former CDA candidates and CDA advisors

- Be flexible and support the needs of your teacher. If, for instance, your program routinely includes worksheets as part of the daily activities, allow your teacher to substitute some type of hands-on alternative, for example, sorting, grouping, and measuring with different types of dried beans, rather than a worksheet about numbers one through ten. The Council does not consider worksheets to be developmentally appropriate practice for use in early childhood programs, so your teacher's CDA advisor will not expect to see any.

- If your center routinely provides art in the form of crafts (children assembling precut, preplanned projects, for example, a paper-plate Santa), allow your teacher to do *creative art* with the children when the advisor visits. Creative art is process oriented rather than product oriented, allowing children free expression and creativity with no predetermined outcome, for example, a collage. Crafts are not considered developmentally appropriate practice by the Council and your teacher's CDA advisor will not expect to see them being done.

- Don't put your teacher into another classroom or age group once she has begun the CDA process. She needs to be in the same room consistently until the verification visit so the families are familiar enough with her to complete the Parent Opinion Questionnaires. Also, your teacher has sent for and received a CDA application packet for a specific setting and is gearing all of her work around that format. All of her work would be invalid in a different setting with a different group of children. She would need to send for a different application packet at an additional cost, redo some of the Professional Resource File, and rewrite all of the Competency Goal Statements. Don't do this to your candidate!

- The candidate may need copies of some of the forms you use at your center for the Professional Resource File. Ask what is needed and how you can help.

- If your center has a file of community resources (for example, names and phone numbers of state, local, or national agencies) that support families, share this with the candidate. Some of the information may be needed for her Professional Resource File.

- Ask your teacher when she plans to send the application to the Council so you can complete the director's portion (section 7) of the application form on time.

- After your teacher has had the formal assessment observation by the CDA advisor and has participated in the verification visit, do not expect her to answer your questions about how she did or to divulge any specific information to you. The Council has a strict confidentiality policy which, if compromised, could jeopardize your teacher's CDA Credential.

- When your teacher finally receives her CDA Credential, offer your sincere congratulations and suggest that she frame the certificate and display it proudly in your center. It will serve as a constant reminder of her commitment to professional excellence and tangible evidence of your center's commitment to providing the best possible care for young children.

The next chapter will explain what happens after the candidate's verification visit has been completed and the CDA Credential has been awarded. You'll also find out what steps to take in the unlikely event the candidate does not meet the Council's criteria for a credential.

Award of the CDA Credential

AFTER THE VERIFICATION VISIT, you will need to wait for a response from the Council. A majority of the time, this response will be in the form of receiving your CDA Credential in the mail.

Sometimes a candidate does not meet the Council's criteria for the CDA Credential for one reason or another. In those situations, the Council will send a letter indicating this and offer you the opportunity to appeal the decision, as well as information about what happens next.

This letter will *not* indicate for what reason, specifically, you did not meet CDA standards. In other words, it will not say that you answered too many questions wrong on the Early Childhood Studies Review or made some incorrect responses during the oral interview or that the Professional Resource File had some items missing. Instead, the Council will tell you only in which of the thirteen Functional Areas you showed some weakness.

Because this is such a generalized response, to prepare for another attempt at the verification visit and a CDA Credential, you will need to review all of your documentation, revising and making improvements where necessary. It may be wise to let an early childhood professional, perhaps someone who has already been awarded a CDA Credential, look over the materials and provide some suggestions.

The next chapter will provide you with the information you need to renew your CDA Credential, which must be done within an allotted amount of time. You will also learn how to get a Second Setting CDA Credential if you have experience in a setting other than the one you used for your initial CDA Credential.

Where Do You Go from Here?

Completing the CDA process and being awarded the CDA Credential is commendable. It shows your commitment to professional excellence in working with young children. And it doesn't have to end here. You are now in a unique position to continue on your path of professional development by getting your associate's, bachelor's, or even master's degree in early childhood education.

If you took courses toward your CDA from an accredited college and earned college credits, you can use them toward your degree. In fact, you can probably continue your course of study with the very same institution. You may want to get an associate's degree through a two-year program. Many two-year community colleges have articulation agreements with four-year institutions within the same state. Upon completing the two-year degree, you are able to move into the four-year program as a junior. At that point, you may decide you want to teach in an elementary school or beyond. Or you may want to continue in your work with children under the age of five. In any case, after only two additional years, you will earn your bachelor's degree.

Paying for additional education does not have to be a roadblock to your future. Many of the state scholarship agencies that were available to help you with your CDA training now have funding in place to assist with degree programs as well. Check with the particular agency you worked with or the child care resource and referral agency in your community for current information about scholarship funding. The college you attend will also be able to help you through its department of financial aid.

As an early childhood professional, you have a personal commitment to lifelong learning. You should look at your CDA Credential not as the end of the road, but as the beginning of your professional journey. Through the CDA process, you have proved your competence and ability to conquer new challenges that lie ahead. Don't let anything or anyone stand in the way of your goals and aspirations. Plan to contact your local community college this week to get information to start working on your degree. You owe it to yourself and to the young children and their families who depend on you.

CDA Renewal
and Second Setting
CDA Credential

11

EARNING A CDA CREDENTIAL INDICATES THAT YOU have achieved recognition in the early childhood profession based on your competency in working with young children and their families. Your CDA Credential can be kept as part of your professional preparation and qualifications indefinitely, as long as it is renewed when required.

More than likely, you spent one or two years in the CDA process taking classes for the required training hours, being observed by an advisor, writing the Competency Goal Statements, assembling the Professional Resource File, and finally participating in the verification visit. If you allow your credential to expire, you will lose what you worked so hard to attain.

If your credential is not renewed within the allotted time limit and it expires, you will have to begin the process all over. No one wants to let that happen, but every year many people do. With a little foresight, commitment, and a calendar, this can easily be avoided.

The CDA renewal process allows you to reaffirm your competence, as well as acknowledge your affiliation with early childhood professionals who are dedicated to providing quality care for young children.

How Often Must My CDA Be Renewed?

If this will be your first renewal, it should be done before the third-year anniversary date. Fortunately for those who forget or procrastinate, the Council has allowed a two-year grace period beyond the three years, giving CDAs a total of five years to renew. Let's say your credential was issued on October 7 five years ago. If your renewal application is received on October 8, just one day past the five-year anniversary date, you are, as they say, a day late and a dollar short!

If this is your second, third, fourth (or more!) renewal, it should be done before every fifth-year anniversary date. Again, the Council allows a two-year grace period, giving seasoned CDAs a total of seven years to renew—*but not a day more!*

Unfortunately, the Council no longer sends out reminders or renewal packets automatically. You must keep track of the expiration date and make a note to yourself to renew. The best policy is to plan to renew before the actual expiration date, and not to plan to use the grace period at all. Better safe than sorry!

Getting a Renewal Packet

To order a renewal packet, call the Council at 800-424-4310 or visit the Council's website at www.cdacouncil.org.

You may remember having experienced a long wait for your original CDA application packet after it was ordered. This may have been due to a high volume of requests, a back order, or some other warehouse problem. Keep in mind that this could also happen when ordering your renewal packet. Allow plenty of time before your CDA expires to order and receive your renewal packet, fill out the application, assemble the required documentation, and send everything back to the Council. I suggest that you allow at least *three months*.

What's in the renewal packet?

When you receive your renewal packet, it will contain these materials:

1. The CDA renewal application form. You fill out the top part of the form. The bottom part is to be completed by the early childhood education reviewer.

2. A CDA Renewal Procedures booklet.

3. An Information for the Early Childhood Education Reviewer booklet.

4. Waiver Request forms.

5. A listing of national early childhood membership organizations.

What's Involved in the Renewal Process?

Renewal is a seven-step process:

STEP 1. *Select an early childhood education reviewer to complete a letter of recommendation to enclose with the application.*

You will ask someone who has firsthand knowledge, within the past year, of your skills and abilities working with young children to be your reviewer. This person can be a coworker, a center director, an early childhood coordinator, or a member of an early childhood organization to which you belong. The person you choose must have training in early childhood or child development and have direct experience with programs for young children. Specifically, she must meet all of the requirements in one of these three categories:

a. A bachelor of arts, bachelor of science, or advanced degree in early childhood education/child development or home economics/child development from an accredited college or university, including twelve semester hours covering children from birth through five years. In addition, the individual must have two years of experience in a child care setting serving children from birth through five years. During this time, one year needs to have been spent as a caregiver or teacher working directly with children in the same age range as the children in your classroom and one year spent being responsible for the professional growth of another adult.

b. An associate's or two-year degree in early childhood education/child development or home economics/child development from an accredited college or university, including twelve semester hours covering children ages birth through five years. The individual must also have four years of experience in a child care setting in a program serving children birth through five years. During this time, two years must have been spent working directly with children in the same age range as the children in your classroom as a caregiver or teacher and two years must have been spent being responsible for the professional growth of another adult.

c. An active CDA Credential, including twelve semester hours of study in early childhood education or child development at an accredited college or university covering children from birth through five years. This individual will also have six years experience in a child care setting serving children from birth through five years. During this time, four years must have been spent as a caregiver or teacher working with children as in the same age range as the children in your classroom and two years must have been spent being responsible for the professional growth of another adult.

The Council will consider waiving certain requirements if the potential reviewer has other qualifications or experience. The reviewer must submit a written explanation and documentation of alternate formal and informal training related to early childhood education/child development and experience in early childhood teacher preparation. There is a Waiver Request form in the CDA Renewal Procedures booklet for this purpose. This form may either be mailed or faxed to the Council:

The Council for Professional Recognition
2460 16th Street NW
Washington, DC 20009-3547
Fax: 202-265-9161

The reviewer you choose must not be in these roles:
- Working with you as a co-teacher in the same room or group on a daily basis
- The relative of a child in your care at any time during the renewal process
- Related to you by blood or marriage or other legal relationship

Any of these situations would be considered a conflict of interest and would interfere with the reviewer's objectivity and credibility.

The person acting as your reviewer will be expected to read over the CDA Competency Standards and thirteen Functional Areas in the Information for the Early Childhood Education Reviewer booklet. After doing so, she will complete the recommendation form, also found in this booklet. The reviewer will then check one of the following choices:
- I strongly recommend this CDA for renewal.
- I recommend this CDA for renewal.
- I recommend, with reservations, this CDA for renewal.

The reviewer is given space on the form (and can also use a separate sheet, if desired) to describe your performance with children in relation to the six CDA Competency Goals and the thirteen Functional Areas.

Finally, the reviewer will sign the form, as well as complete some identifying information. The reviewer will then return the form to you in a sealed envelope. The reviewer will also need to fill out and sign the bottom half of your CDA renewal application form.

STEP 2. *Show proof of current first-aid certification.*

You will need a current Red Cross, Green Cross, American Heart Association, or local hospital first-aid certificate. You will enclose a photocopy of the certificate with your application.

STEP 3. *Show proof of 4.5 continuing education units (CEUs) or a 3-credit-hour course, which equates to approximately 4.5 CEUs.*

One CEU is ten contact hours of participation in an organized continuing education experience under responsible sponsorship, capable direction, and qualified instruction. The 4.5 CEUs would represent forty-five contact hours of instruction.

These training hours must have been earned *since* you obtained your CDA Credential and not be part of your initial CDA training. You will send a photocopy of a college transcript or of your CEU certificates with your application. *All CEUs and college coursework must have been completed within the past five years.*

You may obtain CEUs through participation in several types of training, including in-service and association-sponsored workshops. To be accepted, these training sessions or workshops must award CEUs. They must be documented in the form of a certificate or transcript issued by an agency or organization with expertise in early childhood teacher preparation. College coursework and CEUs may be obtained at vocational/technical schools, community colleges, or two-year and four-year colleges and universities.

To meet this requirement, you must have completed all the coursework in early childhood/child development and should cover one or more of the following subject areas:

1. Planning a safe, healthy learning environment

2. Steps to advance children's physical and intellectual development

3. Positive ways to support children's social and emotional development

4. Strategies to establish productive relationships with families

5. Strategies to manage an effective program operation

6. Maintaining a commitment to professionalism

7. Observing and recording children's behavior

8. Principles of child development and learning

STEP 4. *Show active status as a caregiver.*

To revalidate your CDA Credential, you need to have maintained your competency in working with young children. Therefore, you are required to maintain a current relationship with young children even if you no longer work directly with children. Within one year prior to your renewal, you must have a minimum of eighty hours of work experience with young children. If your employment no longer involves working with young children, there are other ways of meeting the requirement. These might include visiting an early childhood setting as a helper or volunteer, organizing and conducting a family event or workshop with children, or planning a field trip.

To verify the hours you have worked, have someone familiar with your work, preferably a supervisor, write a letter confirming the number of hours. This letter will be submitted with your application form and other documentation. The person you ask to do this could be a coworker, a lead teacher, a center director, or someone in a similar role.

STEP 5. *Show proof of membership in a national or local early childhood professional organization.*

You are required to be an active member of a national or local early childhood association. CDAs are expected to demonstrate basic knowledge about young children and their families. They are expected to conduct themselves in an ethical manner at all times. The requirement for CDAs to belong to professional organizations has been in effect since 1996. A list of such organizations is provided in the CDA Renewal Procedures booklet. You will enclose a photocopy of your membership card or other document proving that you have been a member during at least the past year prior to your application for renewal.

STEP 6. *Collect all documentation and completed forms, along with the $50 renewal fee.*

STEP 7. *Mail everything to the Council.*

We suggest sending these materials via certified mail, return receipt requested. That way, you will not only have proof of mailing but also receive a postcard indicating that your envelope was received. You will mail your materials to this address:

The Council for Professional Recognition
2460 16th Street NW
Washington, DC 20009-3547

What Happens After the Council Receives My Renewal Application?

When your materials have been received, the Council will review them. If the materials you sent are incomplete (perhaps you forgot to enclose something), the Council will notify you and you'll have the opportunity to correct the problem. Since this will obviously delay your renewal for months, it's best to double-check that everything is in order and completed before you mail your materials. The CDA Renewal Procedures booklet has a handy checklist for everything you'll need to send in with your application form. Use it!

If everything is complete and all requirements are met, the Council will award the CDA Renewal Credential, which is valid for five years. When you receive it, mark your calendar as a reminder for your *next* renewal, so you won't inadvertently overlook it.

Earning a Second Setting CDA Credential

The Council offers the Second Setting CDA Credential to center-based and family child care CDAs. As a second setting candidate, you would need to do the following:

- Document a minimum of forty-five clock hours of training specific to the second setting. The hours may be part of the original 120 formal training clock hours or additional training.

- Have a minimum of sixty clock hours of work experience with children of the second setting or age group. These hours must be accrued over a period of no less than three months within the past five years while you are working as a volunteer or paid staff in a group setting.

- Be observed by an advisor of your choosing in a program in which you are working as a lead caregiver with the second setting or age group.

- Compile a Professional Resource File consisting of seventeen resource items, six Competency Goal Statements, and an autobiography, all specific to the second setting or age group.

- Distribute and collect Parent Opinion Questionnaires from the parents of the children in the second setting or age-group class.

Here is some additional information about acquiring a Second Setting CDA Credential:

- The fee for the Second Setting CDA Credential is $325 as of 2011. Please be sure to check with the Council in case this fee has changed.

- There will *not* be a verification visit with a Council representative. The candidate will be required to send all materials directly to the Council.

A Bilingual Second Setting CDA Credential is available for those who obtained their original credential with a bilingual specialization. Home Visitor CDAs may apply for a Second Setting Credential but must complete the direct assessment process and pay the reduced fee of $225.

Detailed information about obtaining a Second Setting CDA Credential and the application materials are available by contacting the Council at 800-424-4310.

CDA Subject Areas for the 120 Clock Hours of Training

WITHIN THE PAST FIVE YEARS, CDA candidates must have completed 120 clock hours of formal child care education, with at least ten hours in each of the eight subject areas listed below. This requirement may be met through participating in a variety of options available, including in-service training and coursework at a college or university. The examples provided will help you determine which of the subject areas have been covered by a training session or course and how many clock hours were devoted to each. This breakdown will need to be indicated on the Direct Assessment Application form.

Subject Areas	Examples
1. Planning a safe, healthy learning environment	Safety, first aid, health, nutrition, space planning, materials and equipment, play
2. Steps to advance children's physical and intellectual development	Large- and small-muscle development, language and literacy, discovery, art, music, mathematics, social studies, science, technology, and dual-language learning
3. Positive ways to support children's social and emotional development	Adult modeling, self-esteem, self-regulation, socialization, cultural identity, conflict resolution
4. Strategies to establish productive relationships with families	Parent involvement, home visits, conferences, referrals, communication strategies
5. Strategies to manage an effective program operation	Planning, record-keeping, reporting, community services
6. Maintaining a commitment to professionalism	Advocacy, ethical practices, workforce issues, professional development, goal setting, networking
7. Observing and recording children's behavior	Tools and strategies for objective observation and assessment of children's behavior and learning to plan curriculum and individualize teaching, developmental delays, intervention strategies, individual education plans
8. Principles of child development and learning	Typical developmental expectations for children from birth through age five, individual variation including children with special needs, cultural influences on development

Title of Course or Training	Total # Clock Hours	Subject Areas							
		1	2	3	4	5	6	7	8

Sample Observation Tool (Anecdotal Record Form)

SEVERAL TYPES OF OBSERVATION TOOLS can be used to record information about a child's behavior. Among them are checklists, time samplings, running records, and anecdotal records. Professional Resource Collection item 16 asks that you locate an observation tool used in recording information about children's behavior. If you do not have one of your own, you might want to recreate the sample anecdotal record provided here.

An anecdotal record is a type of observation tool. It is a short, written record based on observations of a child's behavior. It is recorded during the course of the day while the child is engaged in his or her regular schedule of activities. An anecdotal record is a written snapshot, taken at one point in time, recording what was seen and heard; it is usually no more than one or two paragraphs in length. These notes include dates, times, and the context in which the observation was conducted, for example, whether indoors or outdoors, which area of the classroom, with whom, engaged in what activity.

Anecdotal records are quite valuable during parent/teacher conferences, when the teacher needs to explain how a child is doing and why. These records also help to justify why the teacher made a particular decision regarding a child and to plan appropriate activities to support his development.

To maintain validity, credibility, and value, anecdotal records must be entirely objective. The purpose of these records is to document behavior, not to provide comment or opinion on it. After the observation is written, there is typically a space at the bottom of the form, separate from the observation recording area, where the observing teacher can make notes and express an opinion or comment, if desired.

You may want to use an anecdotal record as the observation tool for Professional Resource Collection item 16 under

Competency Goal VI. Look over the completed sample observation form to clarify your understanding of an anecdotal record. Then create two copies of a blank form. The Council asks that for item 16 of your Professional Resource Collection you include two copies of an observation tool, one blank and a second that shows your written observation of a child.

Choose a child to observe in your program. Be as inconspicuous as possible while recording the information about what you see and hear so the child will not be influenced by your presence. *Do not indicate the child's name on the form.* Write only what you see and hear. Do not include any personal feelings, opinions, or comments. Save those for the section at the bottom. When your anecdotal record is complete, put it back to back with the blank form in the item 16 page protector of your Professional Resource File.

Observation Tool
Anecdotal Record

Date and time:	Context	Child
September 20 9:30 a.m.	Dramatic play area with 2 other girls, playing restaurant	M. (female) age 3

Observation

M. enters the dramatic play area where L. and D. are playing restaurant. M. says, "Can I play, too? I can be the waiter or the cooker."
D. answers, "Sure. You can help us cook the eggs."
M. proceeds to get out some pans and spoons. She watches what D. is doing and imitates her. The three girls continue playing together for about 5 minutes.
M. leaves to paint at the easel.

NOTES: M. is making good progress in entering a play situation without being disruptive. She asked if she could join the girls this time, instead of barging into the area and taking over.

C

Sample Individual Weekly Activity Plan for Infants

WEEKLY ACTIVITY PLANS FOR INFANTS are decidedly different than those used for groups of toddlers and preschoolers. This is because caring for infants is highly individualized and the curriculum revolves almost exclusively around their care and routines. The sample form, therefore, reflects one day's activity plan for one specific infant, rather than for all of the infants in the group.

In actual practice, you would complete a form for each individual infant in your care. The activity sections reflect the major areas of development.

For item 4 under Competency Goal I, you are asked to provide a sample of a weekly lesson plan you would use with the infants in your care. Besides listing appropriate activities and goals, you are also asked to indicate the adaptations necessary for children who may have special needs. You may use your own activity plan form or create one based on the form provided here. Since you will be using an activity plan for one specific infant, you will complete it for a child with special needs, either actual or fictitious.

At the top of the sample Individual Weekly Activity Plan for Infants, you will write the child's first initial and a very brief description of her disability. Along with the specific activities and their associated learning goals, describe how you will adapt each activity to enable this child, who has some type of disability, to experience, learn from, and enjoy these activities to the maximum extent possible. For ideas about adapting activities for children with special needs, you will find the following websites helpful:

- Circle of Inclusion, www.circleofinclusion.org/english /accommodating/index.html

- National Network for Child Care, www.nncc.org
- Tots 'n Tech, http://tnt.asu.edu

After looking over the sample form, create two blank weekly forms. Fill in one of them and leave one blank. Put them both in the item 4 page protector of your Professional Resource File.

The sample form shows one day's worth of activities. You will need to create five days of activities, one for each day of the week, for one infant.

Individual Weekly Activity Plan for Infants

Name: K. (female) 8 months
Date: April 6–10
Special Need(s): Developmental delays (low neck and upper body strength)

Monday

Language Development

Activity: Story: *Baby Faces* by Margaret Miller

Say words that name parts of the faces and point to them

Learning Goals: Hearing the names of parts of the face

Adaptation: None needed

Cognitive Development

Activity: Drop the Toy

Take turns dropping the toy to the floor and watch it drop

Learning Goals: Object permanence

Adaptation: Hold K. in lap to keep her in upright position

Creative Development

Activity: Crib Gym

Suspend toys over K.'s feet. Encourage her to kick and move them

Learning Goals: Make objects move with her feet

Adaptation: None needed

Gross Motor

Activity: Tummy Time

Place K. on her tummy. Place toys within her reach

Learning Goals: Raise her head and upper body, reach for toys

Adaptation: Play for short periods of time so she doesn't tire

Fine Motor

Activity: Picking up Cheerios on Tray

Learning Goals: Grasping with her fingers

Adaptation: Extra support

Social Development

Activity: Saying Hello

Place K. on tummy face to face with a friend

Learning Goals: Encourage responses

Adaptation: Play for short periods of time so she doesn't tire, place her on her back and talk with the teacher, and make faces

Sample Weekly Activity Plans for Toddlers and Preschoolers

FOR ITEM 4 UNDER COMPETENCY GOAL I, you are asked to provide a sample of a weekly lesson plan you would use with your group of children. You may use your own form or one based on the samples provided here. One form is for toddlers and the other is for preschoolers. Each form includes a sample plan for one day of the week, Monday. You will need to prepare activity plans for all five days of the week.

The information on the form must include brief descriptions of the activities provided for each of the learning areas. You will need to describe the expected learning goals for each activity, as well as the ways you would adapt the activity for a child with special needs.

You may have a child with special needs in your classroom. If so, briefly indicate the nature of the disability on the form. To maintain confidentiality, do not use the child's name. Instead, use the child's first initial. For each activity, suggest how you could make adaptations that would enable this child to learn, experience, and enjoy it to the maximum extent possible.

If you do not have a child with special needs in your classroom, you will need to create a hypothetical child with a disability. On the form, indicate the child's particular disability and then describe how you would adapt your activities for that child. For ideas about adapting activities for children with disabilities, check out the following websites:

- Circle of Inclusion, www.circleofinclusion.org/english/accommodating/index.html

- National Network for Child Care, www.nncc.org

- Tots 'n Tech, http://tnt.asu.edu

After looking over the completed sample forms, create two copies of blank weekly forms for your particular age-level endorsement. Fill in one of them and leave one blank. Put them both in the item 4 page protector of your Professional Resource File.

The sample form shows one day's worth of activities. You will need to create five days of activities, one for each day of the week, for a toddler or preschooler.

Weekly Activity Plan for Toddlers

Theme: Bubbles
Children with Special Needs: M. has small-motor and sensory impairment.
Date: April 4–8

Monday Activities

Playing with Toys and Materials

Activity: Exploring Bubble Plastic

Under supervision, press and stand on bubble plastic of different sizes

Learning Goal(s): Find out what happens when the bubbles are pressed

Adaptations: Use a block for pressing bubbles

Exploring Art

Activity: Painting on Bubble Plastic

Large brushes on pieces taped to the table, may make prints

Learning Goal(s): Dip brush in paint, brush paint on plastic, enjoy process

Adaptations: Use Velcro fastener to attach brush to hand, assist

Music and Movement

Activity: "Bubbles, Bubbles All Around"

Song/Movement sung to "Twinkle, Twinkle, Little Star"

Learning Goal(s): Follow movement directions in the song

Adaptations: Assist with movement instructions

Dramatic Play

Activity: Blowing Bubbles with Our Puppet Friends

Puppets, soft plastic bubble wands, small plastic pails: pretend to blow bubbles

Learning Goal(s): Remember how we blew bubbles and repeat this with the puppets

Adaptations: Assist with using the puppets

Water, Sand, and Other Media

Activity: Bubbles in the Water Table

Use baby shampoo; include small plastic boats, funnels, and sieves

Learning Goal(s): Sensory experience of the bubbles

Adaptations: Provide small tub for bubbles

Story Time/Language/Literacy

Activity: Story: *Bubbles, Bubbles* by Kathi Appelt

Read the story together, talk about the pictures

Learning Goal(s): Identify the body parts that are mentioned in the story

Adaptations: Provide board book version of this book

Outdoor Play

Activity: Blowing Bubbles

Use rings and large wands, hula hoop

Learning Goal(s): Dip wand, blow or wave, enjoy the process

Adaptations: Wands with Velcro-fastener attachments

Food and Tasting

Activity: Bubbly Apple Juice

Prepare apple juice using sparkling water

Learning Goal(s): Sensory experience of carbonated juice

Adaptations: None required

Weekly Activity Plan for Preschoolers

Theme: Caterpillars
Children with Special Needs: M. has sensory and small-motor impairment.
Date: April 4–8

Monday Activities

Circle Time

Activity: Story: *The Very Hungry Caterpillar* by Eric Carle

Flannelboard Story: Give each child a story piece to add to the story

Learning Goal(s): Recognize the right time in the story to add a particular piece to the board

Adaptations: Assist with placement of piece on board

Art

Activity: Bouncing Caterpillars

Dip inflated balloons in paint and bounce them on large paper to make caterpillars

Learning Goal(s): Hold balloon, dip in paint, and make prints

Adaptations: Use clothespin as a handle

Music and Movement

Activity: "The Little Caterpillar"

Sung to tune of "Itsy Bitsy Spider"

Learning Goal(s): Learn the words, tune, and movements to the song

Adaptations: Assistance with movements

Dramatic Play

Activity: Becoming Butterflies

Caterpillar and butterfly costumes, items of food that the caterpillar ate in the Eric Carle story

Learning Goal(s): Retell the story by acting it out, using costumes and props

Adaptations: Assistance with costume

Science

Activity: Observing a Butterfly

Monarch butterfly caterpillar in our Butterfly Box

Learning Goal(s): Understand the life cycle of this butterfly by observing over time

Adaptations: None required

Math

Activity: Butterfly Count

Count out plastic butterflies to place in cocoon baskets labeled with numbers 1–5

Learning Goal(s): One-to-one correspondence with objects and numerals

Adaptations: Use larger plastic butterflies

Outdoor Play and Gross-Motor Development

Activity: Caterpillar Crawl

Crawling through a fabric tunnel

Learning Goal(s): Learn concept of fast and slow as they crawl through the tunnel

Adaptations: None required

Fine-Motor Development

Activity: Find the Butterflies

Reach in and pull only the butterflies out of a cloth bag cocoon

Learning Goal(s): Discriminate the butterfly shapes from the caterpillar shapes

Adaptations: Use larger shapes

Language/Literacy

Activity: Story: *The Very Hungry Caterpillar* by Eric Carle

Read the story together, talk about the pictures

Learning Goal(s): Follow the life of a caterpillar, predict what will happen next

Adaptations: Give M. the board book version of this book

Glossary

advisor A professional in early childhood education who observes the candidate at work and completes the CDA Assessment Observation Instrument.

bilingual program A bilingual program is one that has specific goals for achieving bilingual development in children; where two languages are consistently used in daily activities; and where parents are helped to understand the goals and to support children's bilingual development.

candidate An individual who has applied for CDA assessment and who has met all eligibility requirements. A CDA candidate coordinates the information collection responsibility of the advisor and ensures that Parent Opinion Questionnaires have been distributed and collected. The candidate also participates in the verification visit with the Council representative.

Child Development Associate (CDA) An individual who has successfully completed a CDA assessment and who has been awarded the CDA Credential. A CDA is a person who is able to meet the specific needs of children and who, with parents and other adults, works to nurture children's physical, social, emotional, and intellectual growth in a child development framework. The CDA conducts herself or himself in an ethical manner. The CDA has demonstrated competence in the CDA Competency Goals through her or his work in a center-based, home visitor, or family child care program. A person who has demonstrated bilingual competence in a bilingual child care program is a CDA with a bilingual specialization.

CDA Assessment Observation Instrument The official form used by advisors to record observations of the candidate in the thirteen Functional Areas.

CDA training Programs that guide, teach, and support individuals interested in a CDA assessment offered by child care programs, colleges, and universities. The CDA assessment system requires educational experiences in early childhood/child development, but these do not have to be CDA training experiences. Whether or not an individual is enrolled in CDA training does not affect eligibility for an assessment.

center-based One of the settings a candidate may choose for CDA assessment. A center-based setting for CDA assessment is defined as a "state-approved child development center." When a candidate chooses to be assessed in a center-based setting, she or he uses the Competency Standards, eligibility requirements, and information collection requirements designed for that setting.

clock hour Sixty minutes.

Code of Ethical Conduct Standards of ethical behavior developed for the early childhood profession by the National Association for the Education of Young Children.

competence Skill or ability to do something well.

Competency Goals General statements of competence that a caregiver should work toward. There are six CDA Competency Goals:

> **I.** To establish and maintain a safe, healthy learning environment
>
> **II.** To advance physical and intellectual competence
>
> **III.** To support social and emotional development and to provide positive guidance
>
> **IV.** To establish positive and productive relationships with families
>
> **V.** To ensure a well-run, purposeful program responsive to participant needs
>
> **VI.** To maintain a commitment to professionalism

Competency Standards Criteria that define the goals and skills that a competent child care provider or home visitor should demonstrate in working with young children. The Competency Standards consist of six Goals, thirteen Functional Areas, and examples of competent behavior. They were developed and validated by the early childhood profession and approved by the CDA Consortium.

conflict of interest A relationship that may interfere with an advisor's ability to be objective in assessing a candidate. The advisor

1. Must not be working as a co-teacher with the candidate on a daily basis in the room or group where the candidate will be observed;

2. Must not be a relative of a child in the candidate's care at any time between information collection and the verification visit; and

3. Must not be related by blood or marriage or have some other legal relationship to the candidate.

Council representative A professional in early childhood education, trained and endorsed by the Council to conduct a verification visit for a CDA candidate.

Credential A written document from an authorizing body showing that a person has met certain standards. The CDA Credential is awarded by the Council to caregivers who have demonstrated competence in the CDA Competency Standards during the CDA assessment process.

Developmental Context The CDA Competency Standards include a Developmental Context for each of the thirteen Functional Areas. It includes a brief summary of children's development and a context for a caregiver's work with children at the different stages of development.

dual-language learners Children who are learning two languages simultaneously or adding a new (second) language to their primary (home) language.

Early Childhood Studies Review The CDA written examination.

endorsement An applicant for CDA assessment in a center-based setting must choose one endorsement for assessment. The age of the children the candidate works with determines whether the endorsement is preschool (three through five years) or infant/toddler (birth to age thirty-six months). Family child care providers and home visitors are assessed on their work with the families and children in their care who may range in age from birth through five years.

family child care One of the settings a candidate may choose for CDA assessment. A family child care setting for CDA assessment is defined as a family child care home that meets at least the minimum level of applicable state and local regulations, where a candidate can be observed working as a primary caregiver with at least two children five years old or younger who are not related to the candidate by blood or marriage or other legal relationship.

formal education Child care training/preparation for work with children and families. A CDA applicant must have completed 120 clock hours of such preparation. The CDA candidate must have had comprehensive instruction in early childhood education/child development in eight subject areas.

Functional Area A category of responsibility that defines a caregiver's role in relation to children. The six CDA Competency Goals are divided into thirteen Functional Areas defined by the following key words: Safe, Healthy, Learning Environment, Physical, Cognitive, Communication, Creative, Self, Social, Guidance, Families, Program Management, and Professionalism. Each Functional Area is defined by a sentence that summarizes competent caregiver behavior.

oral interview A situation-based assessment of the candidate's knowledge of the thirteen Functional Areas.

Parent Opinion Questionnaires The candidate distributes a Parent Opinion Questionnaire to each family that has a child in her or his group or to each family the candidate visits. The questionnaires give parents an opportunity to describe and evaluate the candidates' work from their point of view.

Professional Resource File A collection of materials early childhood professionals use in their work with young children and families. It is divided into three parts: 1. Autobiography, 2. Competency Goal Statements, and 3. Professional Resource Collection.

renewal The process of revalidating a CDA Credential when it expires. The CDA Credential is valid for three years from the date of award. At the end of that period, a CDA can apply for renewal of the Credential. When renewal is granted, the Credential becomes valid for an additional five years.

setting The type of child care program in which a CDA candidate's performance is evaluated. An applicant for a CDA assessment chooses one of the following settings: center-based program, family child care program, or home visitor program. The CDA Competency Standards, eligibility requirements, and information collection responsibilities are different for each setting.

specialization An applicant for CDA assessment has an option to be assessed for a bilingual specialization. The applicant must work in a program where the two languages and cultures are used consistently with adults and children. The applicant must also be able to speak, read, and write in both languages.

Supplemental Observation form Documentation of candidate interacting with children in the age range not represented during the initial observation. Supplemental observations are applicable only to infant/toddler candidates.

trainer A child development/child care specialist who teaches classes, conducts workshops, models activities with children and families, or works with caregivers individually to improve their skills. Many child care programs have staff or consultants who work as CDA trainers. Sometimes a trainer may become a candidate's CDA advisor. However, a candidate is not required to choose a CDA trainer as the CDA advisor.

Waiver Request form Certain eligibility information collection requirements for candidates and advisors may be suspended by the Council. A copy of the form is available in the Council for Professional Recognition's CDA materials.

References

Bailey, Caryn T. 2004. The 2004 National Survey of Child Development Associates (CDAs). Survey results report prepared in collaboration with the Council for Professional Recognition and the Center for Research on the Education of Students Placed at Risk. Washington, DC: Howard University.

Council for Professional Recognition. 2006. *The Child Development Associate Assessment System and Competency Standards for Family Child Care Providers.* 2nd ed. Washington, DC: Council for Professional Recognition.

Council for Professional Recognition. 2010. *The Child Development Associate Assessment System and Competency Standards for Infant/ Toddler Caregivers in Center-Based Programs.* 3rd ed. Washington, DC: Council for Professional Recognition.

Council for Professional Recognition. 2011. *The Child Development Associate Assessment System and Competency Standards for Preschool Caregivers in Center-Based Programs.* 3rd ed. Washington, DC: Council for Professional Recognition.

Subject Index

C

caregiver roles
    active status, maintaining, 176
    family child care settings, 91–92
    infant/toddler settings, 55–56
    preschool settings, 23

CDA advisors. *See* advisors

CDA Assessment System and Competency Standards books
    copyright date, 18
    cost, 159
    family child care settings, 18, 92
    infant/toddler settings, 18, 56, 159
    preschool settings, 17, 23–24, 159

CDA Credential
    for center-based program directors, 160–161
    continuing education units (CEUs), 175
    Council committee decisions, 15, 169
    eligibility requirements, 4
    expiration, 171
    failure to qualify for, 15, 169
    historical perspective, 1–2
    importance and benefits of, 3, 157
    lifelong learning and, 170
    number of caregivers with, 2
    obtaining information about, 7–8
    renewal, 16, 171–177
    Second Setting Credential, 6, 177–178
    state recognition, 2
    training subject areas, 3–4, 52, 179
    types of endorsements and settings, 6–7
    verification of training, 5, 53, 88–89, 123
    waiver requests, 4, 53, 89
    See also application process

CDAs. *See* Child Development Associates (CDAs)

center-based program directors
    CDA Credential for, 160–161
    Direct Assessment Application form, section for, 53, 167
    frequently asked questions, 158–166
    self-study of functional areas, 161–166
    supporting CDA candidates, 157–158, 166–167

center-based programs
    overview, 6
    advisor eligibility requirements, 9–11
    See also infant/toddler settings; preschool settings

centers, classroom, 48, 83, 118

certificates of training, 5, 53, 88–89, 123

CEUs. *See* continuing education units (CEUs)

challenging behavior, children with, 29, 61, 97–98

child abuse and neglect, reporting, 25, 57, 93

Child Care Services Association, 5

child care settings. *See* family child care settings; infant/toddler settings; preschool settings

Child Development Associate National Credentialing Program, 1–2

Child Development Associates (CDAs)
    defined, 1
    demographics, 2
    See also CDA Credential

circle activities
    adapting for children with disabilities, 184–185, 187
    program tips, 49–50, 85, 120, 163

Circle of Inclusion (website), 184, 187

classroom environment. *See* learning environment functional area

clock hours
    documenting, 52–53, 88, 122–123
    sample form, *180*
    subject areas, 3–4, 179

Code of Ethical Conduct (NAEYC), 53, 89, 123

cognitive development competency goal/functional area
    family child care settings, 95–97, 108
    infant/toddler settings, 59–60, 72
    preschool settings, 26–28, 38–39
    program director self-study items, 163–164
    program tips, 49, 84, 119
    sample activity, 59–60, 96

college courses
    continuing education units (CEUs), 175
    recommended topics, 4
    using toward degrees, 170

communication development functional area
    family child care settings, 109
    infant/toddler settings, 72–73
    preschool settings, 39
    program director self-study items, 164

community agencies. *See* agencies

Competency Goals
    organizing and labeling resources, 18, 24–34, 56–66, 92–103
    program tips based on, 47–51, 81–87, 117–121
    summary, 8

Competency Goal Statements
    Council checklist and scoring, 129
    family child care settings, 103–114
    infant/toddler settings, 66–78
    preschool settings, 34–44
    timeline for submission, 14
    word count, 129

confidentiality
    Council policy, 127, 167
    Parent Opinion Questionnaires, 20
    program directors and, 127, 167

conflicts of interest
    advisors, 12
    reviewers, 174